PARDON MY FRENCH COLORING:

a sweary adult coloring book with cursing in french, italian, spanish, and british english

BY FIFI LA SWEARY

This book is dedicated to Nick, whose cursing is always classy and on point.

ARTIST'S NOTE

Thank you for buying this book. I hope it helps you cope with difficult days, and if you are going through a tough time, that it brings you many hours of coloring pleasure and relaxation.

This coloring book is the result of months of work, from researching the words themselves to learning how to publish a book. I drew the images, digitized every page, then compiled them electronically to prepare a quality book for printing. I have officially registered this book with the Copyright Office. Don't be a *comemierda* – please respect Copyright Law.

You are welcome to:

Remove and/or copy the uncolored pages on other paper preferences for yourself only.
Post colored images on social media.
Give the colored pages as a gift.
Give a physical book you purchased as a gift.

Only fils de pute would:

Share physical or electronic copies of uncolored pages with anyone else.
Post uncolored pages anywhere online, claim them as your own, distribute uncolored pages via e-mail.
Incorporate uncolored or colored images on items besides printed pages.
Sell colored images from this book, use them on products, or for any commercial usage.

PardonMyColoring.com   Facebook.com: Pardon My French Coloring

ISBN-13: 978-1533219657
ISBN-10: 1533219656

THIS BOOK BELONGS TO:

_____

ABOUT THIS BOOK

I was drawing a coloring book page at the end of a particularly difficult day, and the day's page was not cutting it. A sweary page would fit the day's feelings so much better, and looking at the blank page, a French curse word came to mind. Thus the idea for this book was born, and I drew the image that is now on the cover of this book that same night. I worked on this book during difficult days and I finished it before the other one I was working on!

My home is in the United States, but I have visited countries where the words in this book are commonly spoken: I have been to Paris and a few other French cities multiple times; visited Rome, Italy and Madrid, Spain; Lived in both London and Oxford in England; and lived for years and traveled in Latin America as well. I speak three and a quarter languages: English, Spanish, French, and some basic Italian. Whenever anyone learns that I speak a foreign language, questions always arise about foreign curse words. One thing I have learned throughout my travels is that curse words seem to be used more casually in Europe than they are in the United States and Latin America. Exercise care where you use these words, because they can range from a slightly sassy way of saying "dude" to nuclear level insults and filth depending on the location and context where they are used. Latin America in particular is so diverse that although I chose fairly universal Spanish curse words, their exact meanings and levels of filth may vary in different countries.

I made these coloring pages in a variety of styles and levels of complexity to address a variety of life situations, from basic annoyances such as when someone cuts you off in traffic (simple designs that are quick to color pages) to tough situations such as difficult breakups, bad neighbors, or a boss from hell, that require you to get lost in coloring for hours (full size complex designs.) I made the designs available full and half size so you could have twice as much fun and would be able to color more easily when you don't have as much time to color.

The purpose of these coloring pages is to make you chuckle and help you relax and cope. To get the maximum fun out of this book, don't worry about making the final colored pages perfect. This paper is particularly good for coloring pencils, but don't let that limit you. Designs were printed single sided to address bleed through. If you're using markers, slip a couple extra pages or a sheet of cardstock behind the page you're working on so you don't curse because those markers you used bled through to the next image. Most importantly, have fun coloring these naughty filthy words in 4 different languages! There is a glossary in the back of the book to help you expand your sweary vocabulary.

I'd love to see how you color your pages and to hear what they are helping you to cope with. I am already working on the second volume, so if you have any requests or suggestions, please feel free to visit my site, find my Facebook link, and share them - who knows, you may find I added your favorite foreign curse words to the next volume! So visit my site PardonMyColoring.com to share your work, get coloring tips, find a link to my Facebook page, and to find out when the next book is out!

À bientôt and happy coloring!

Fifi La Sweary

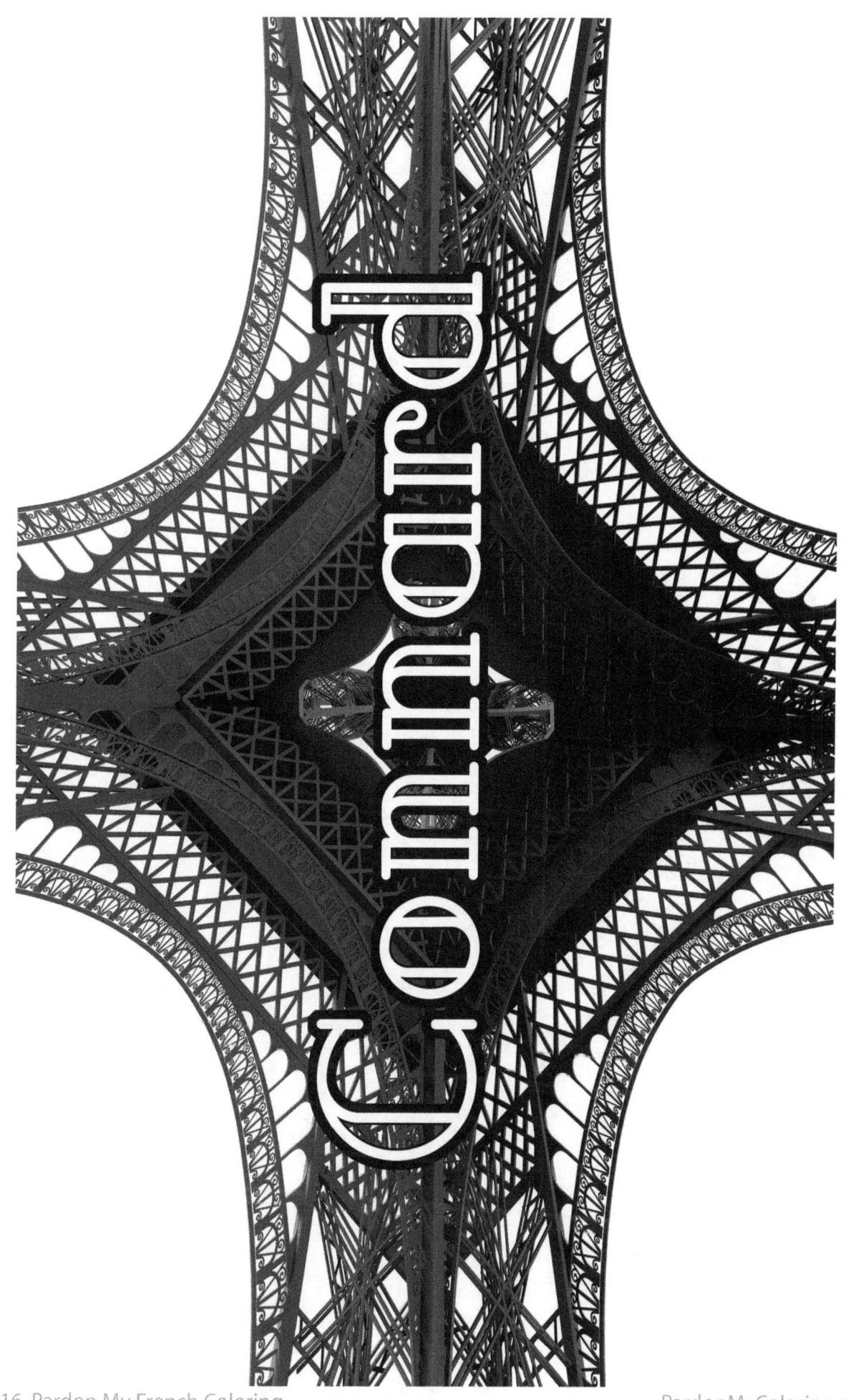

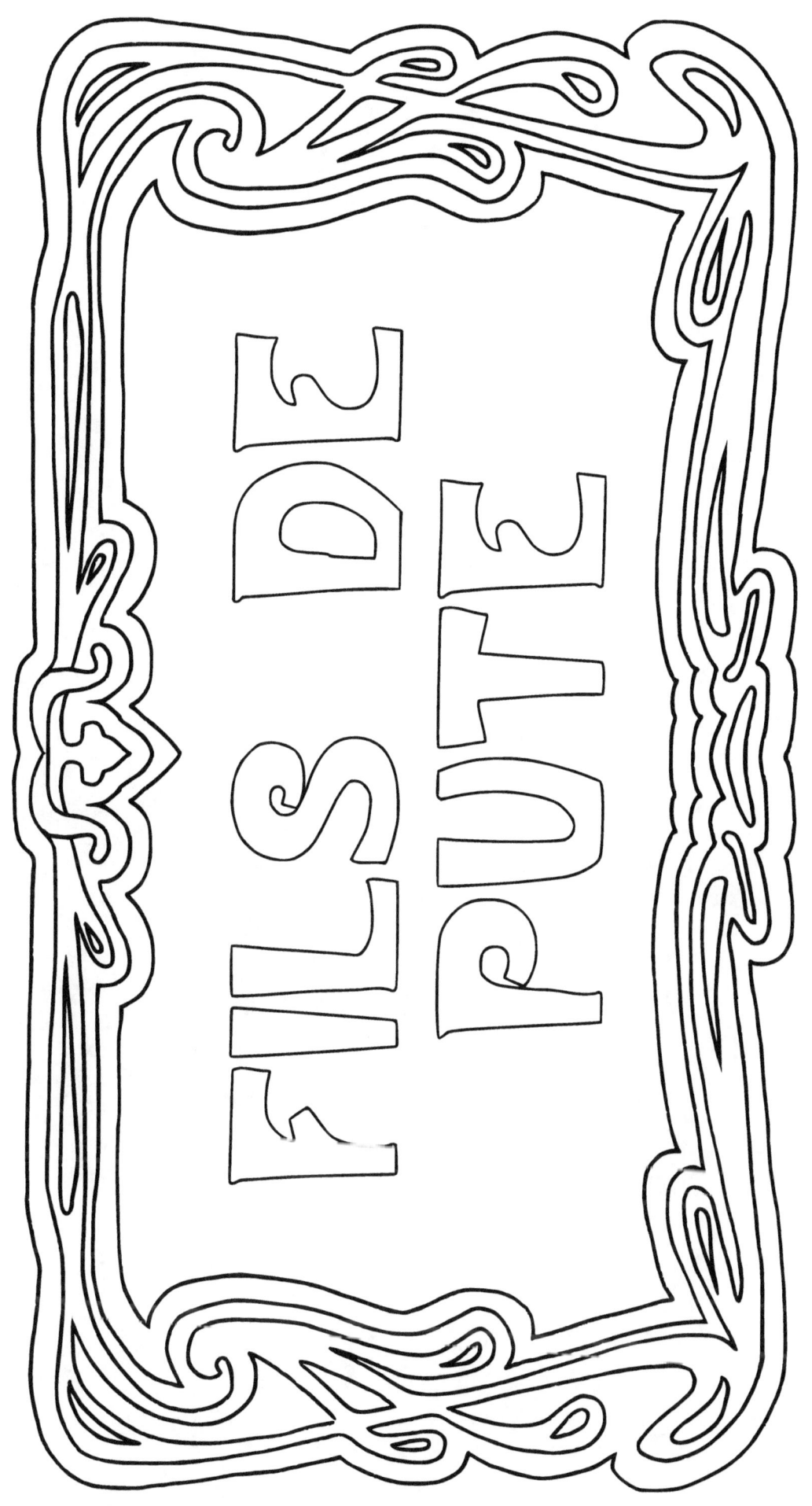

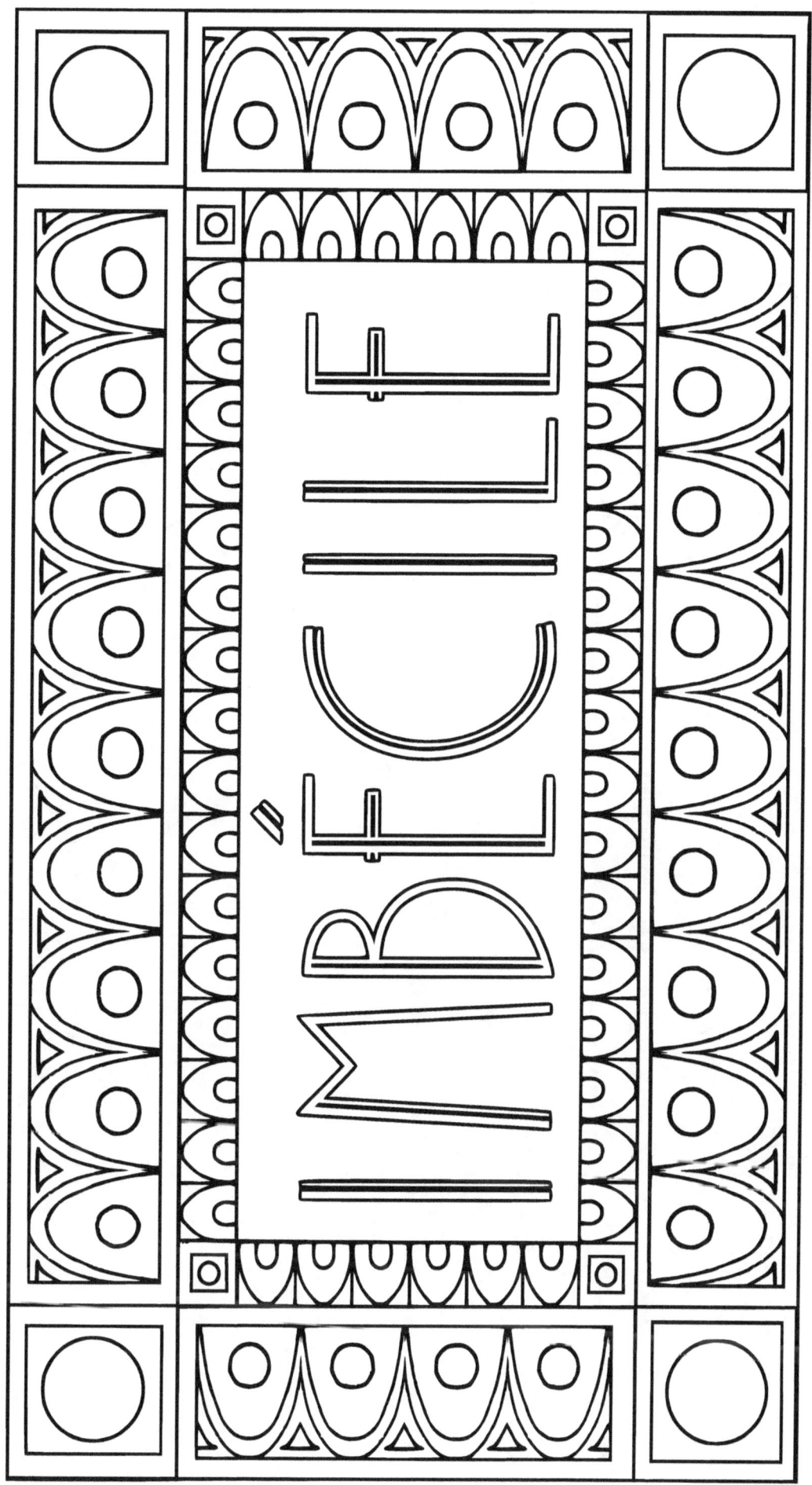

Je m'en fous

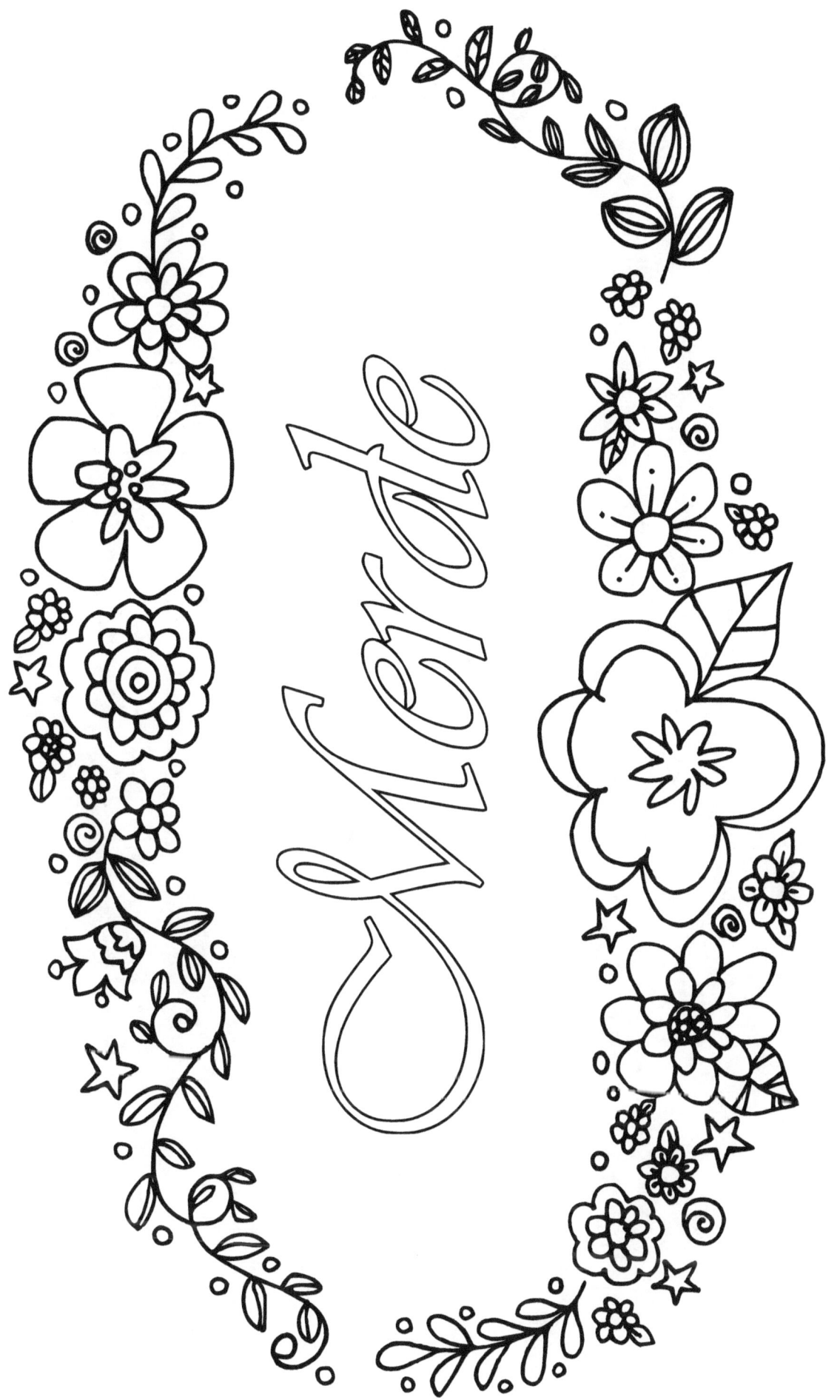

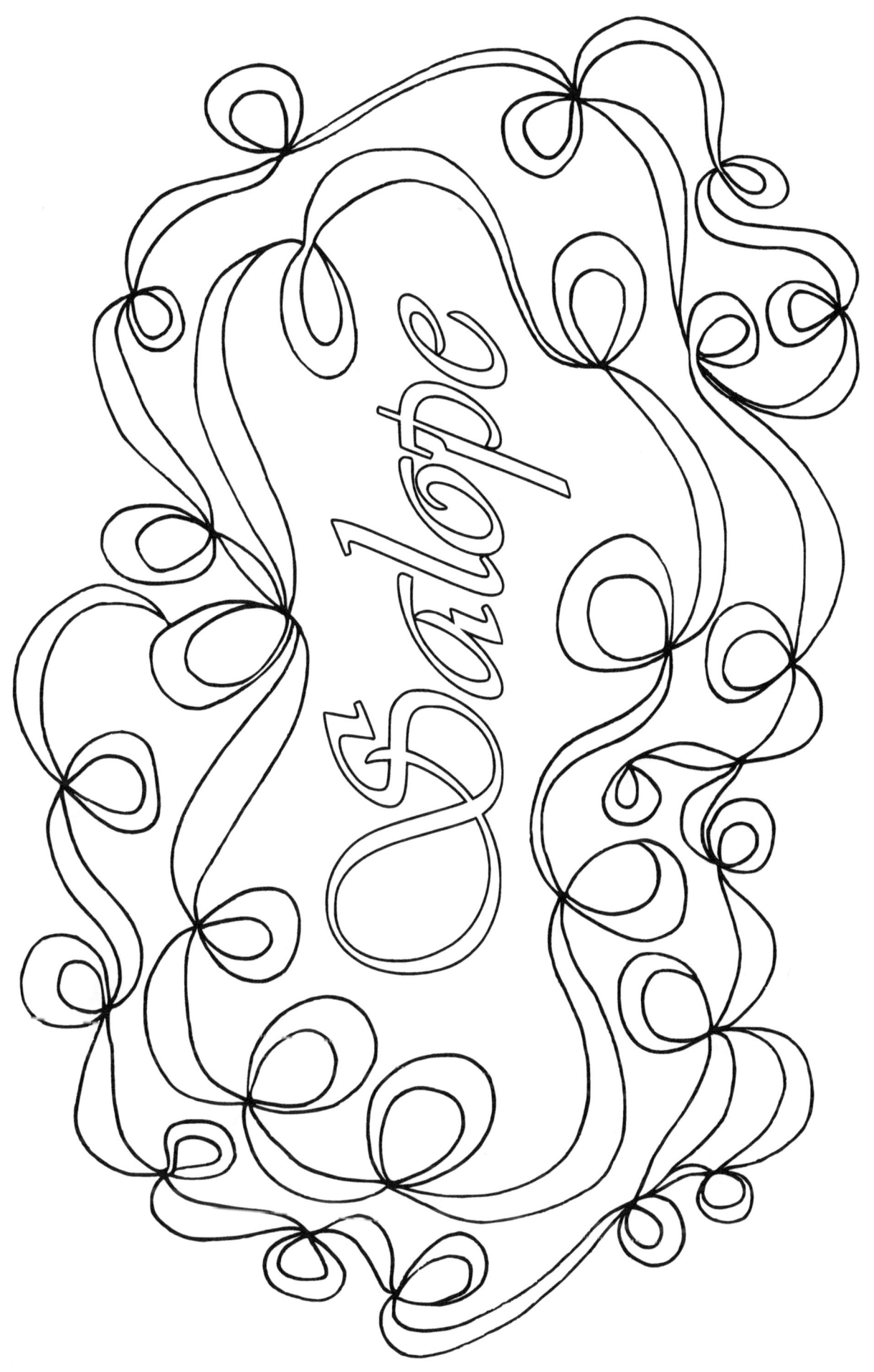

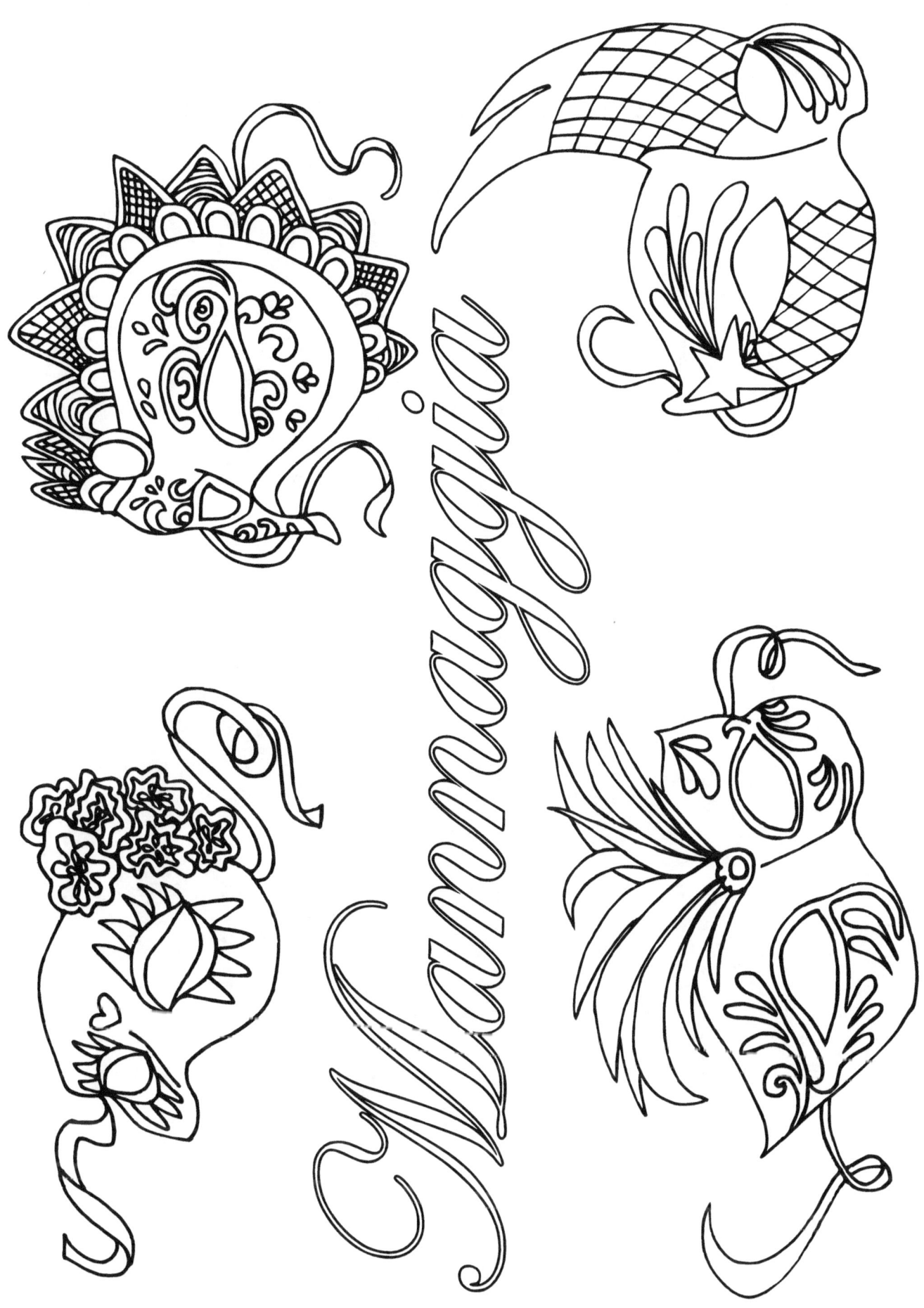

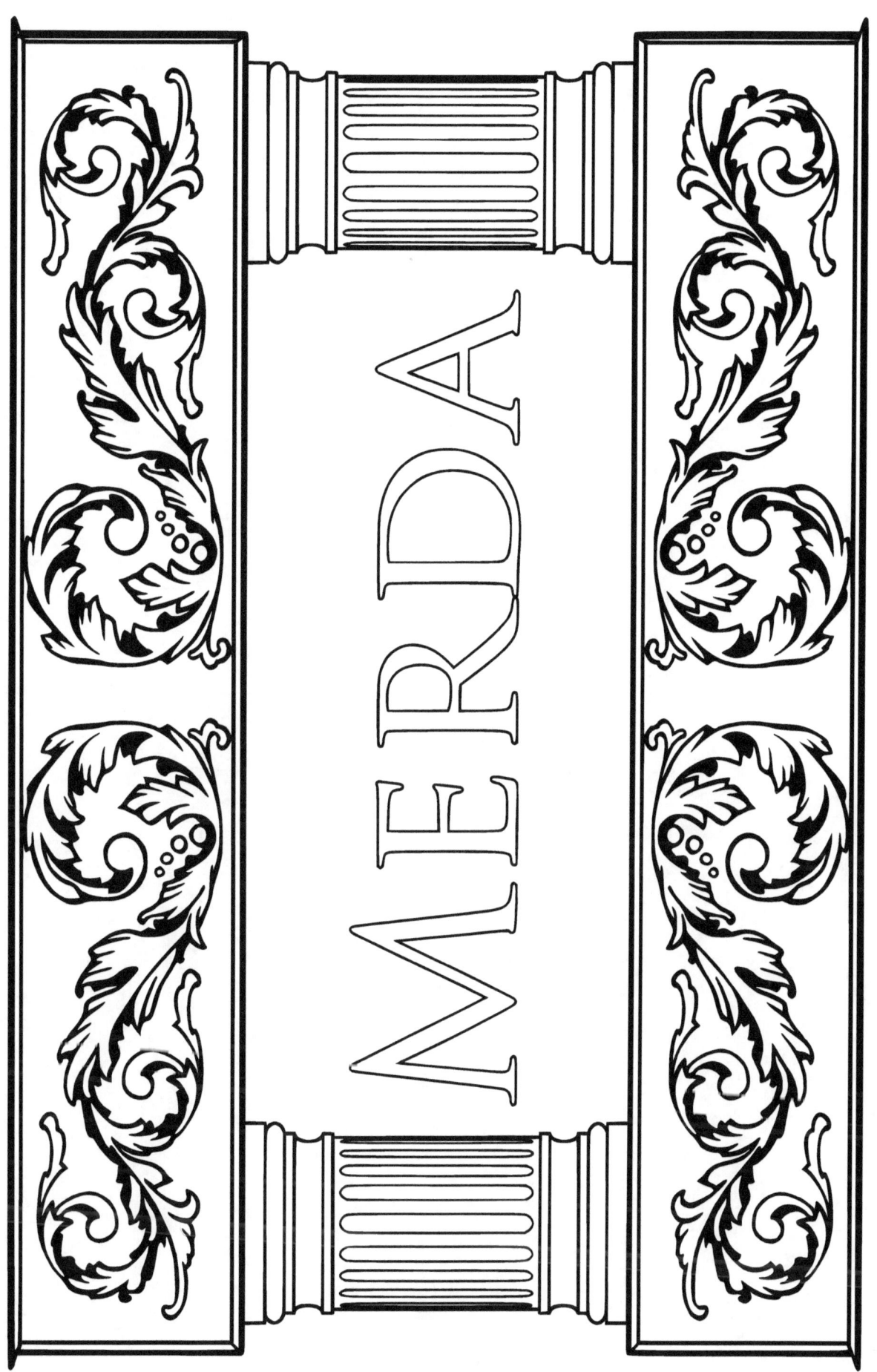

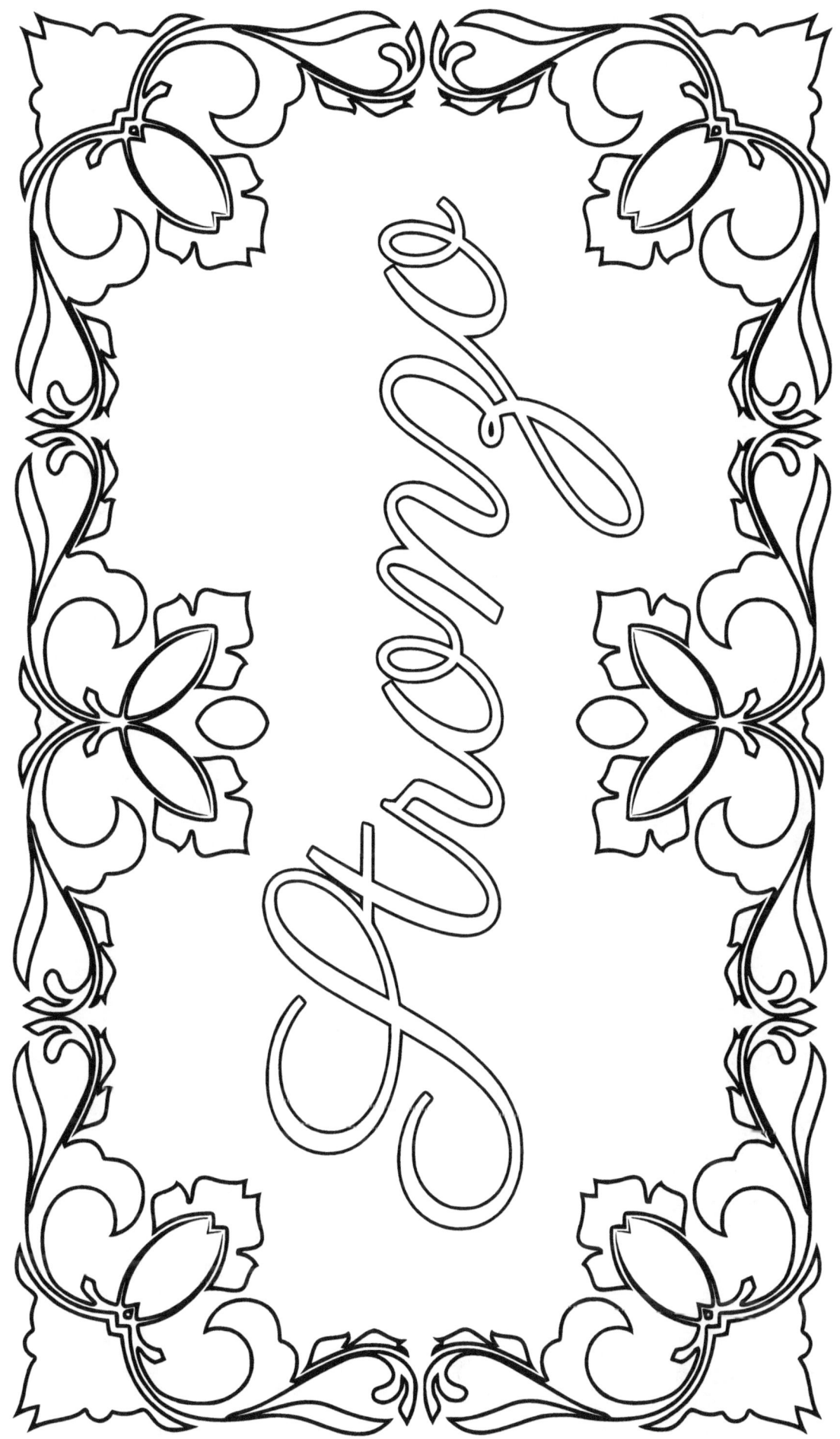

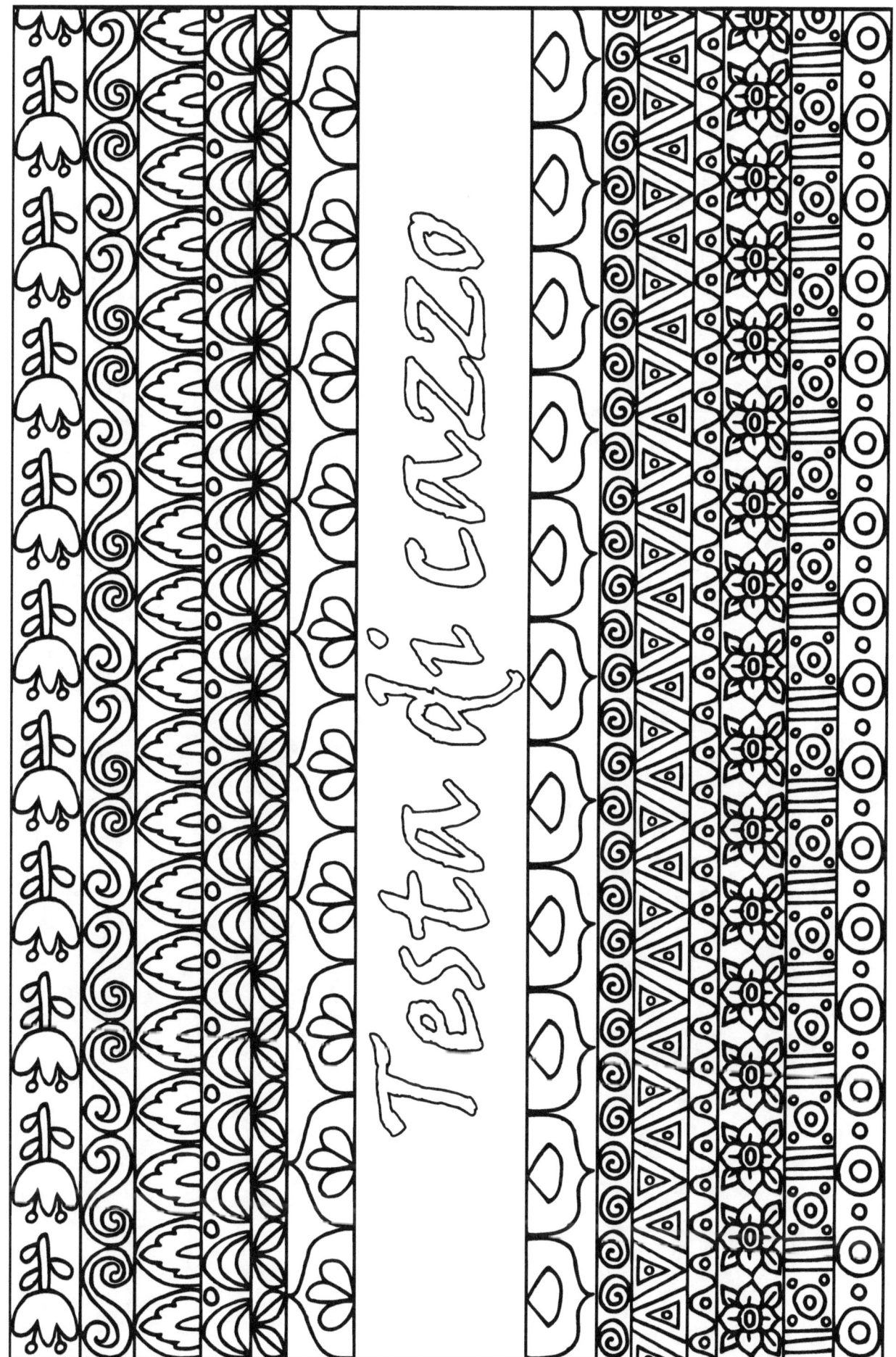

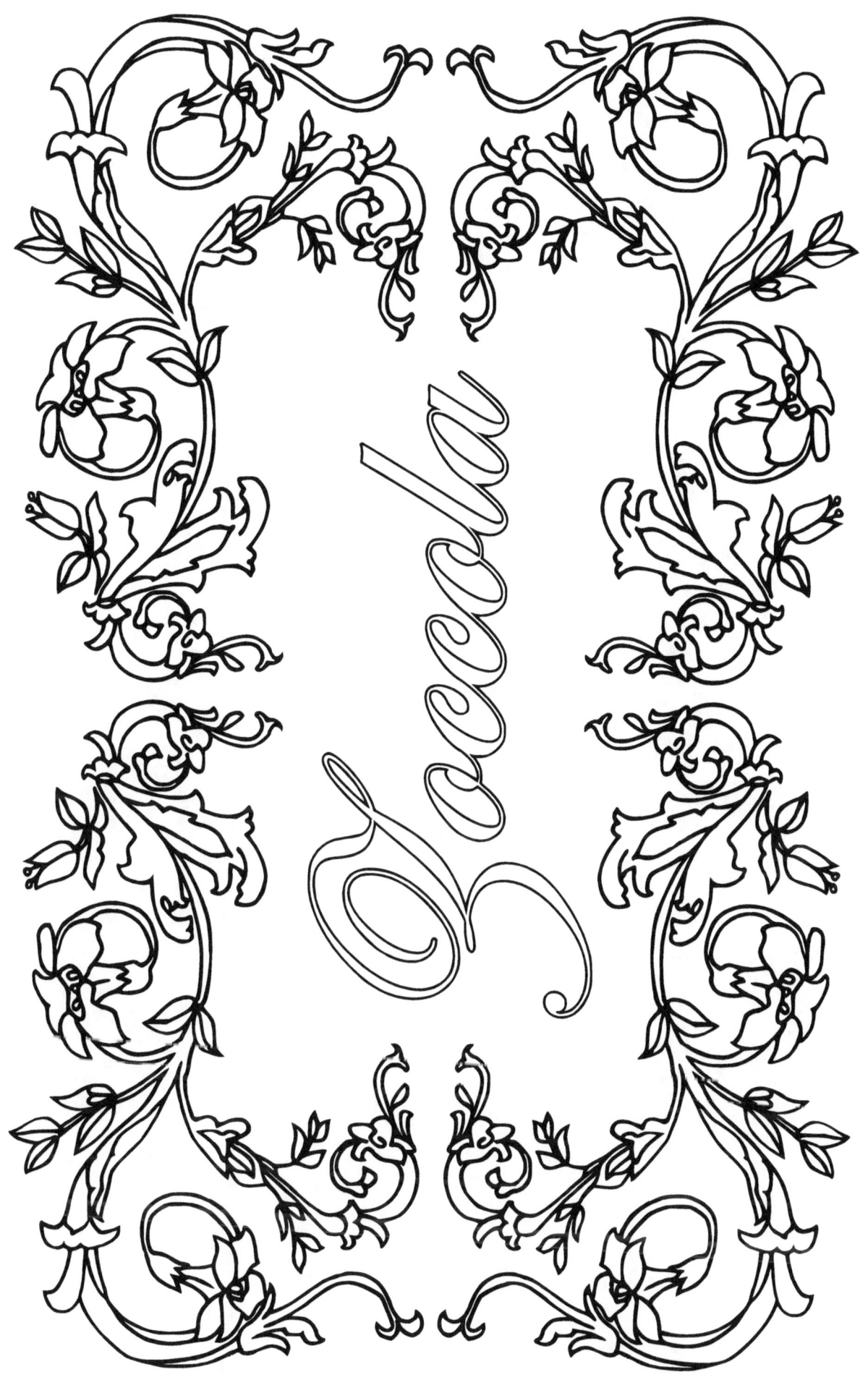

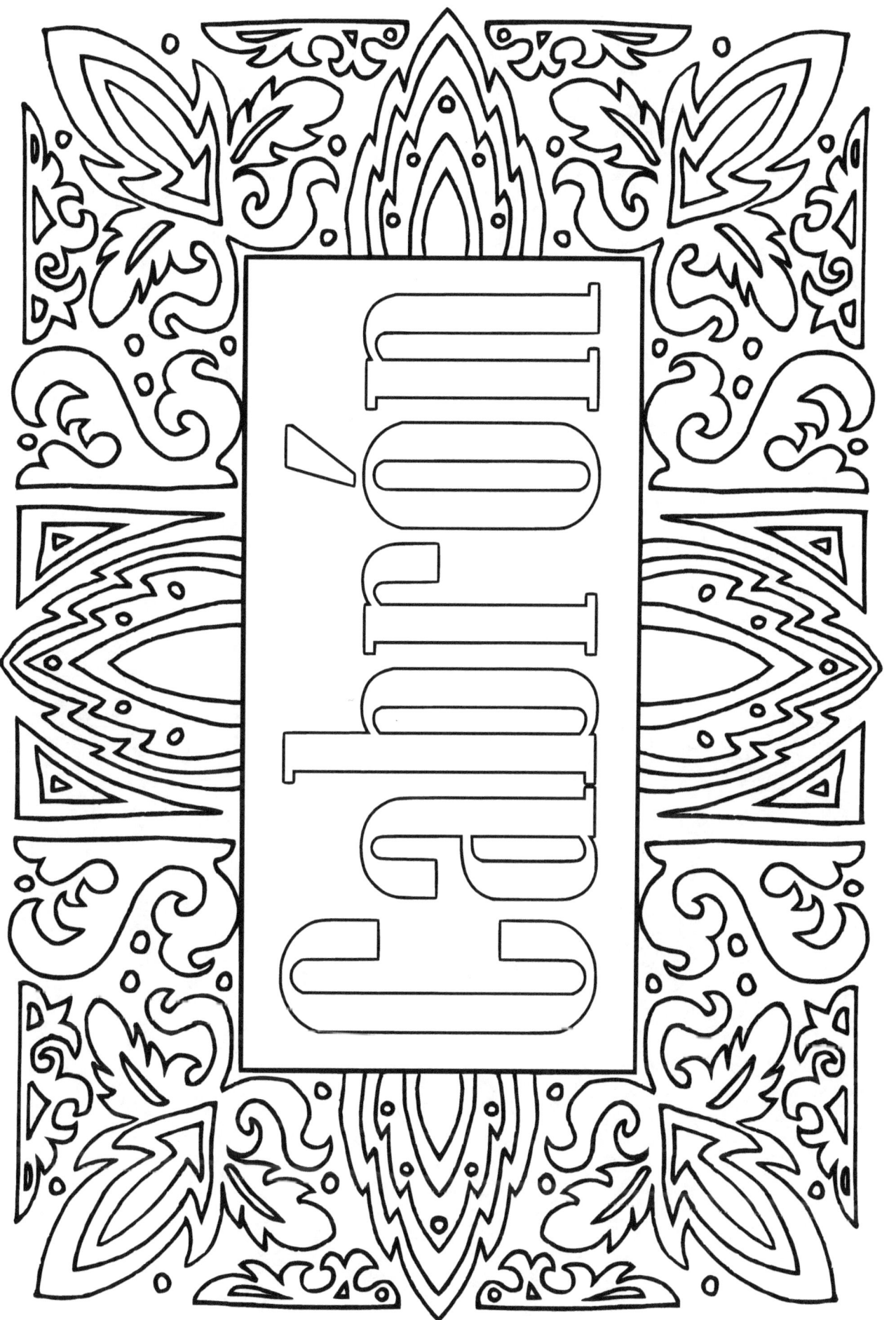

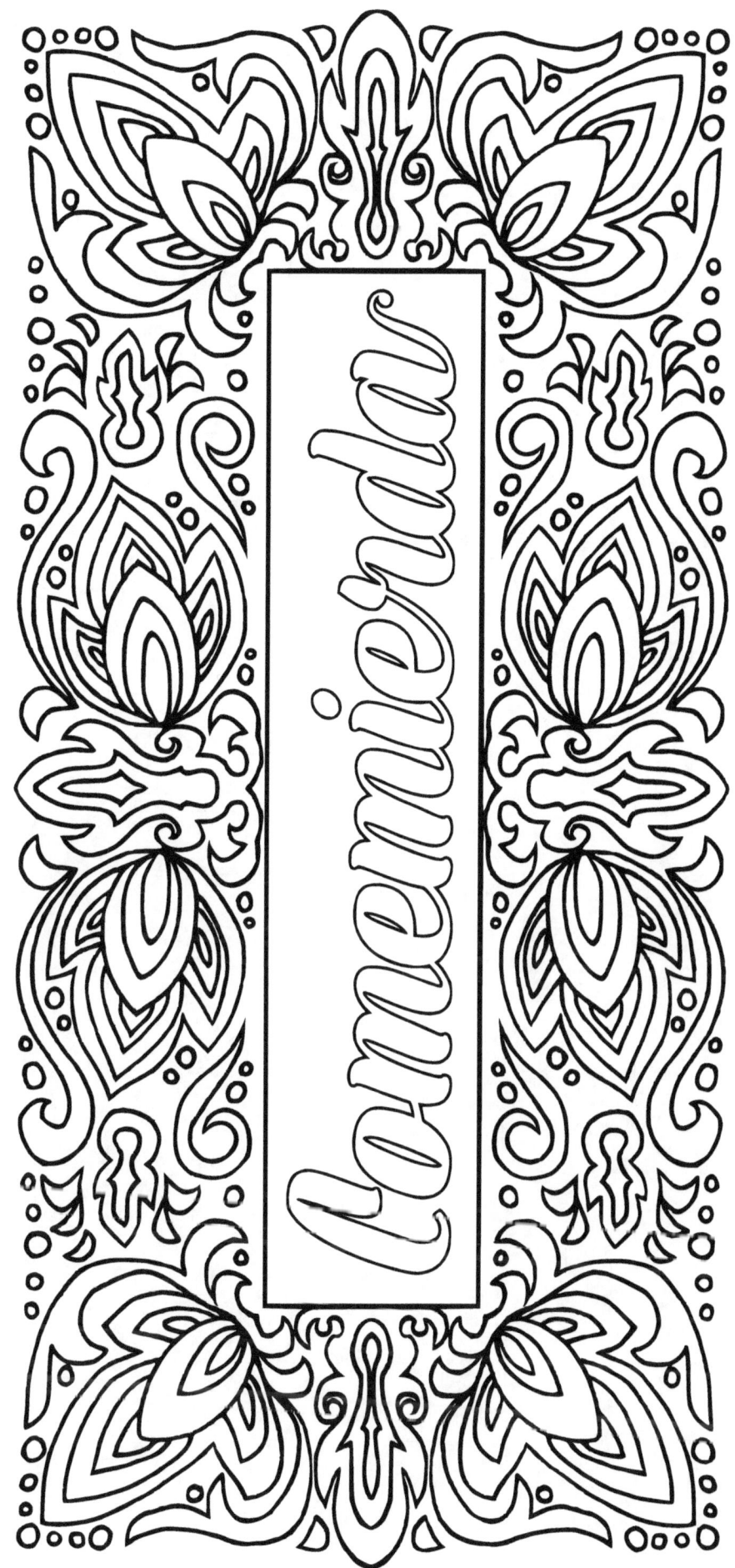

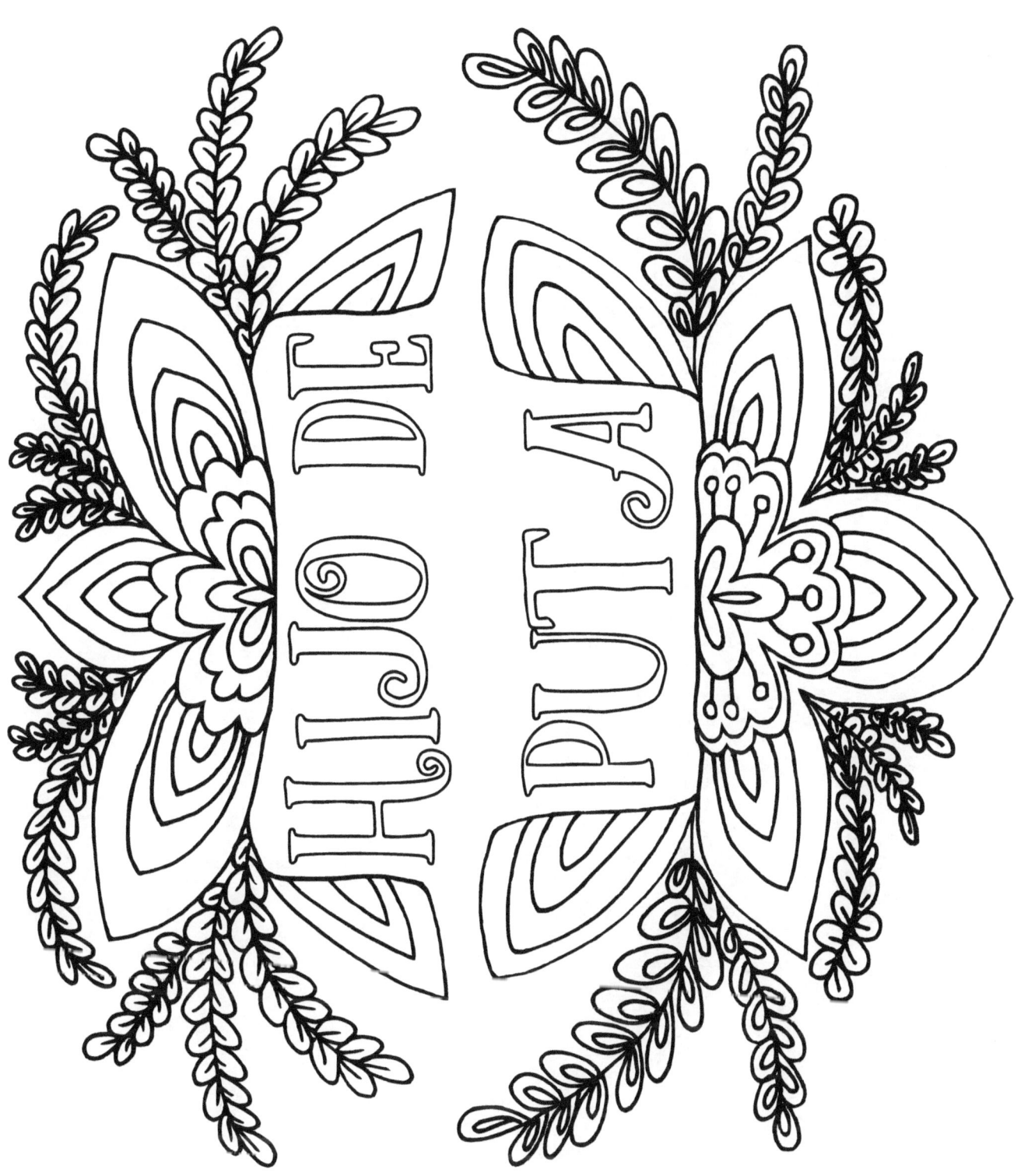

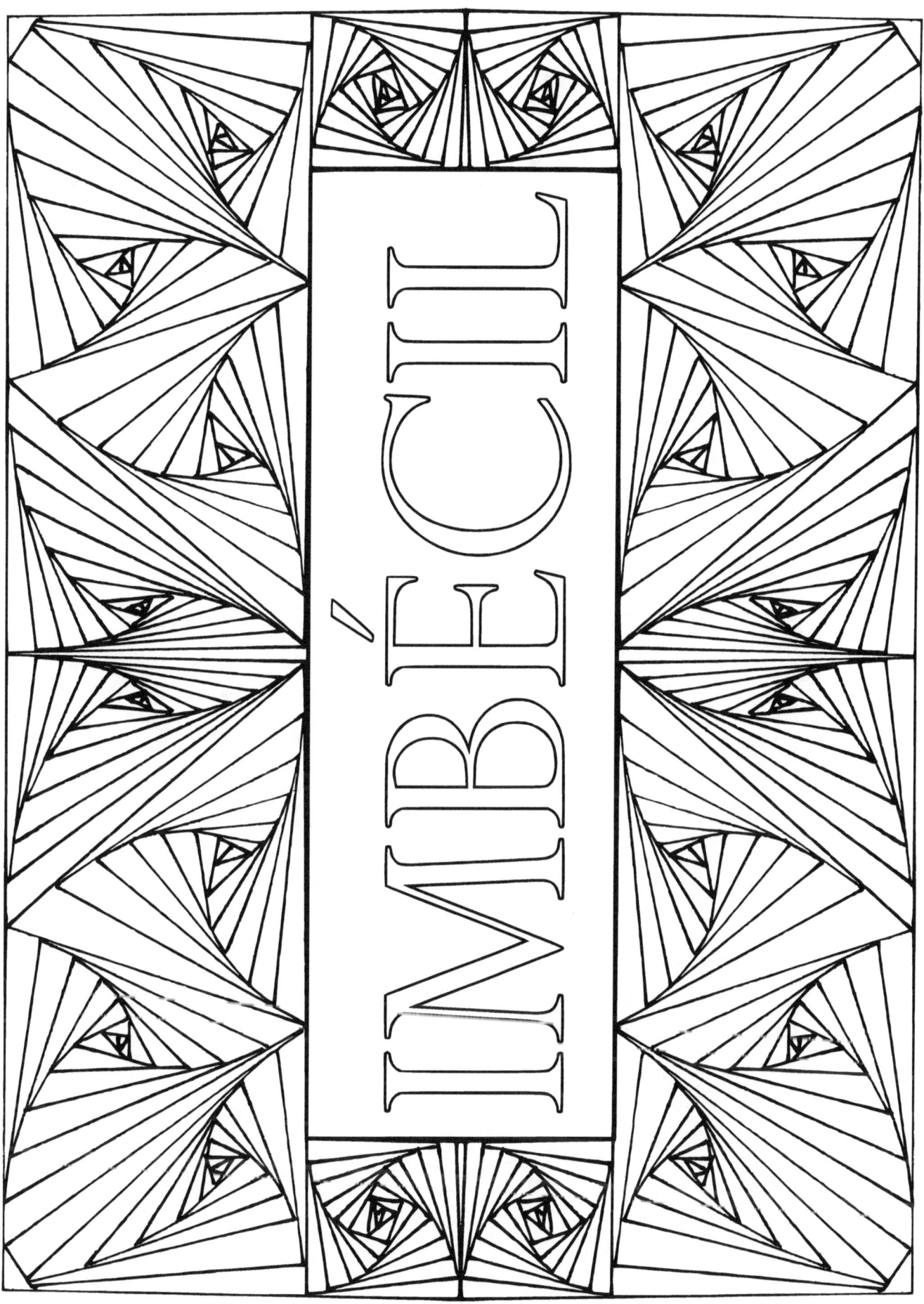

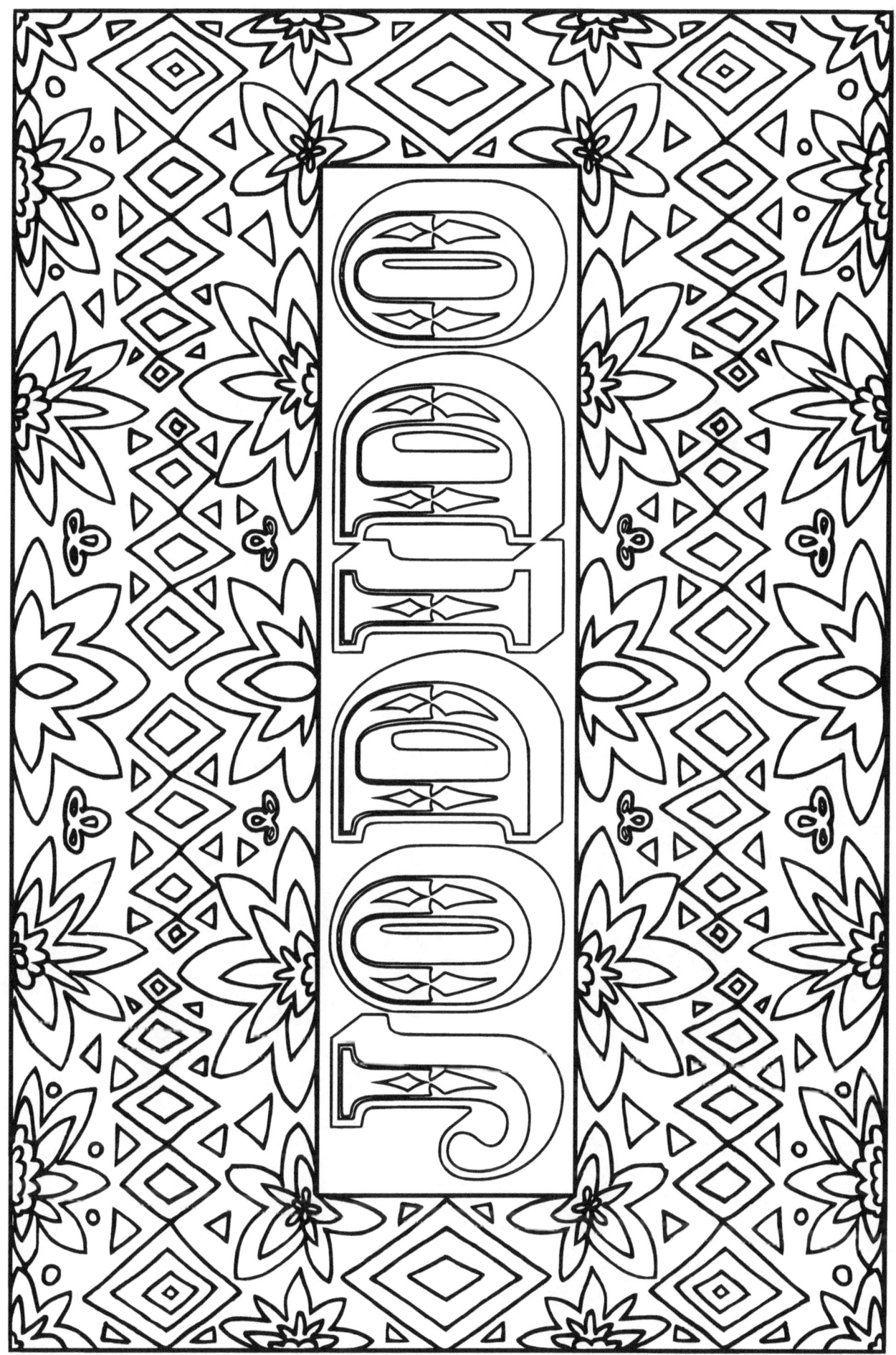

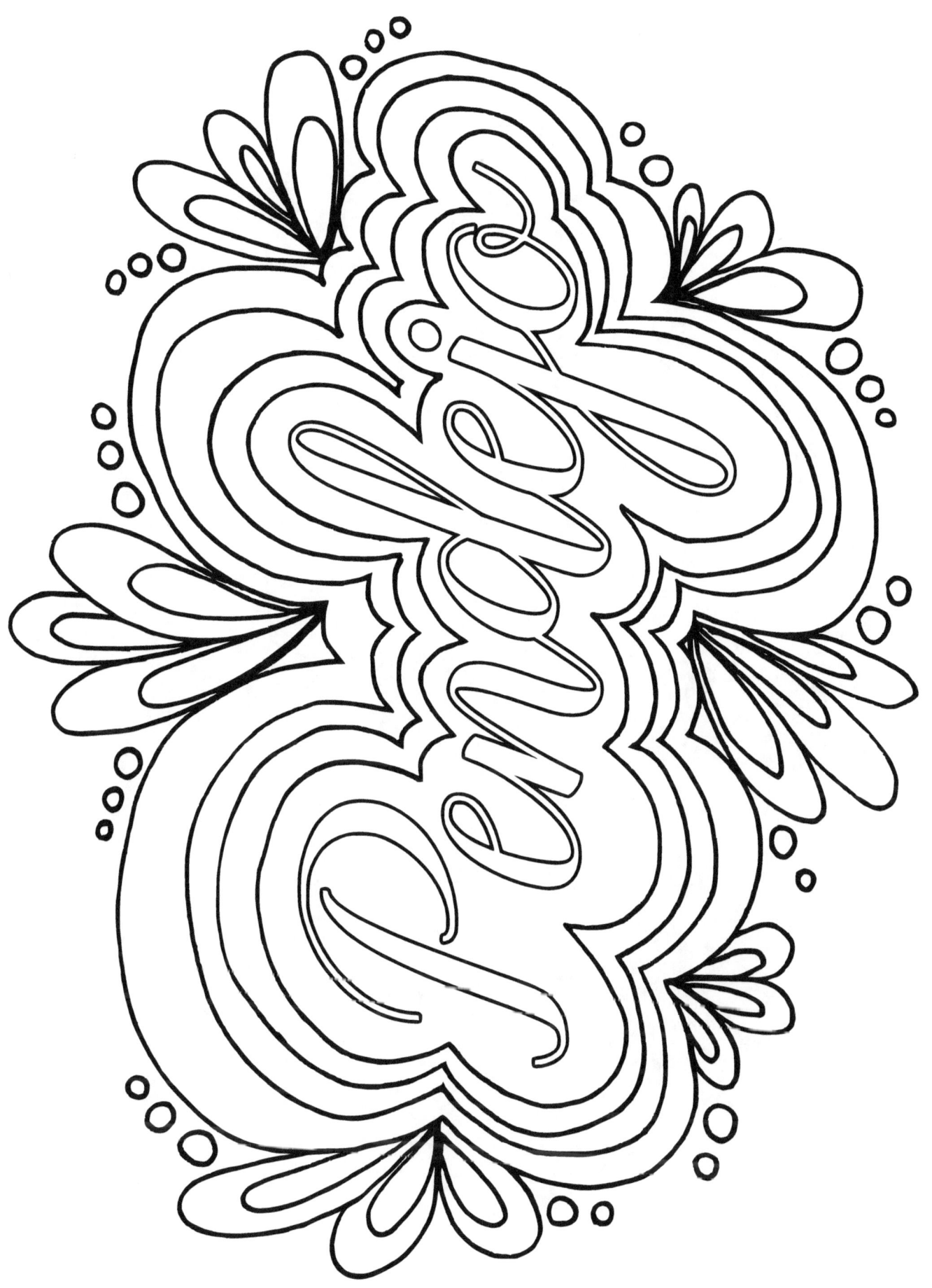

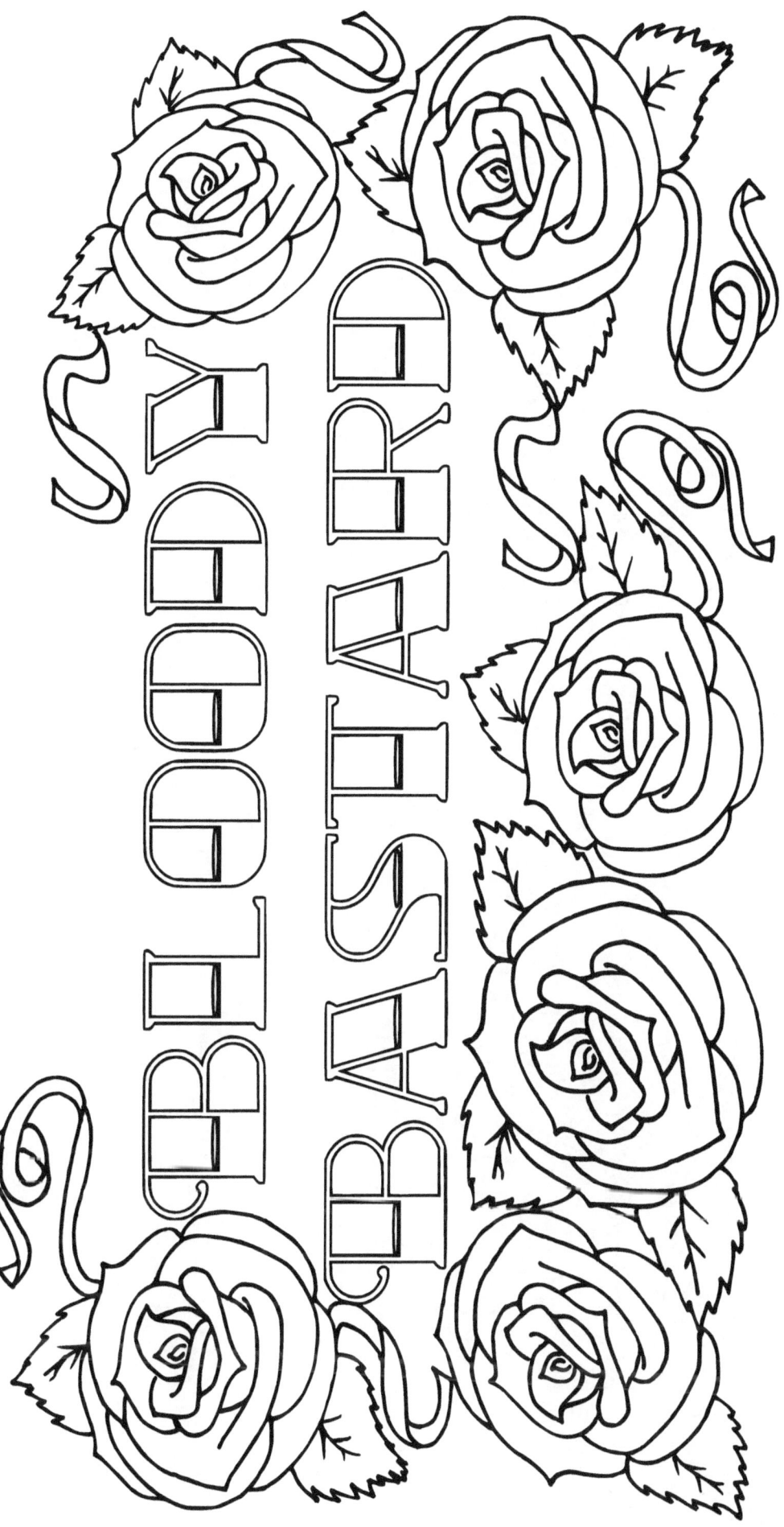

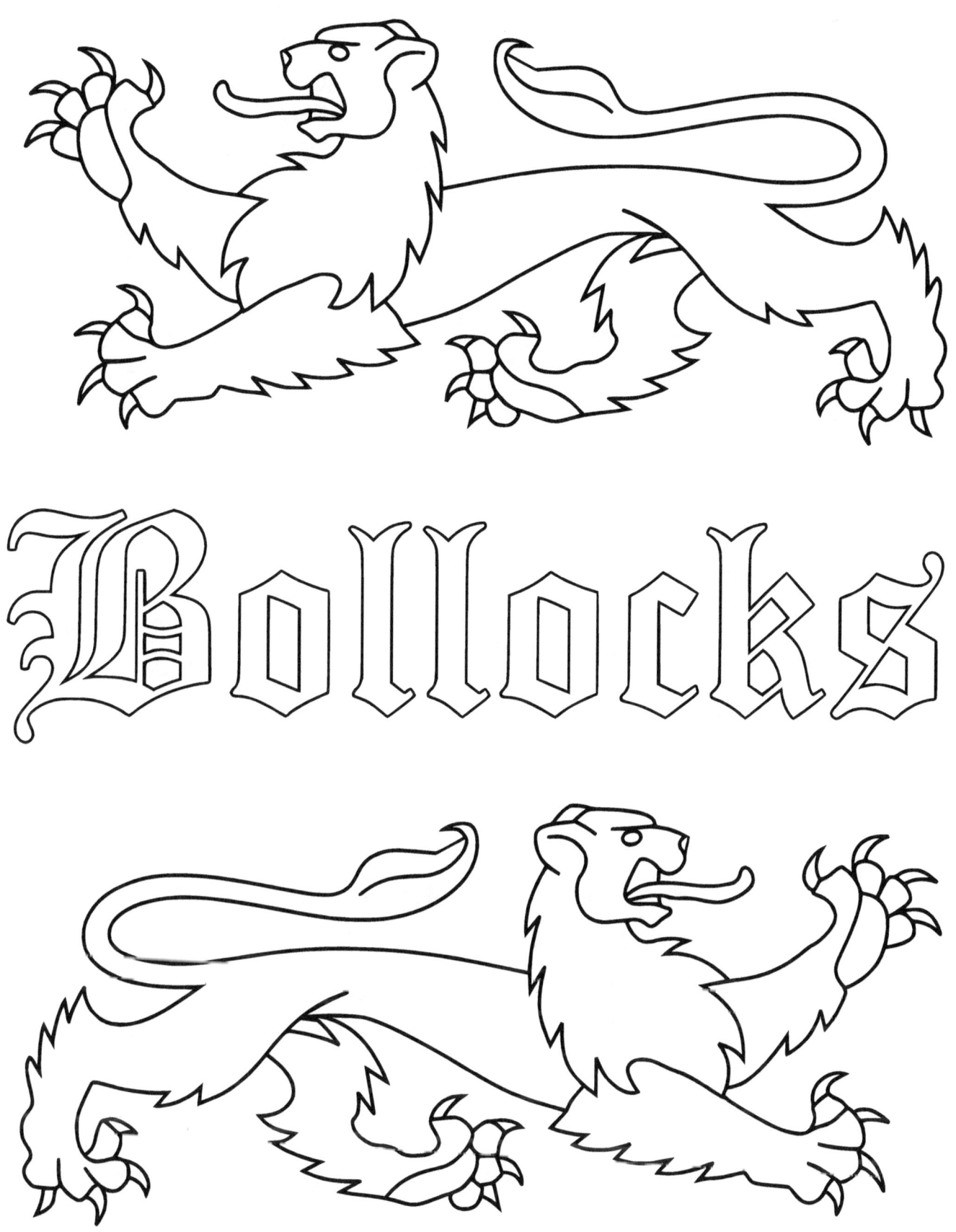

Bollocks

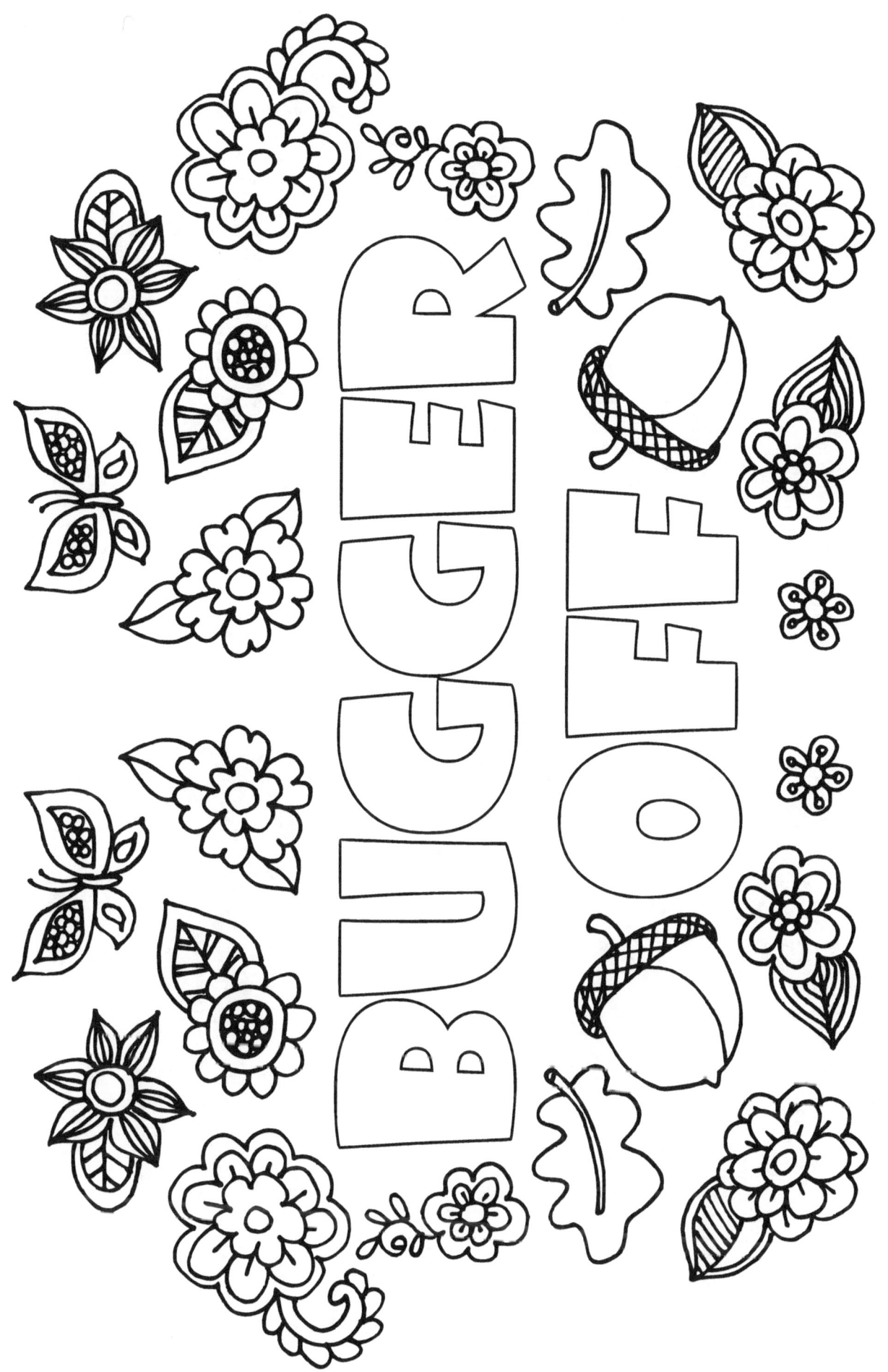

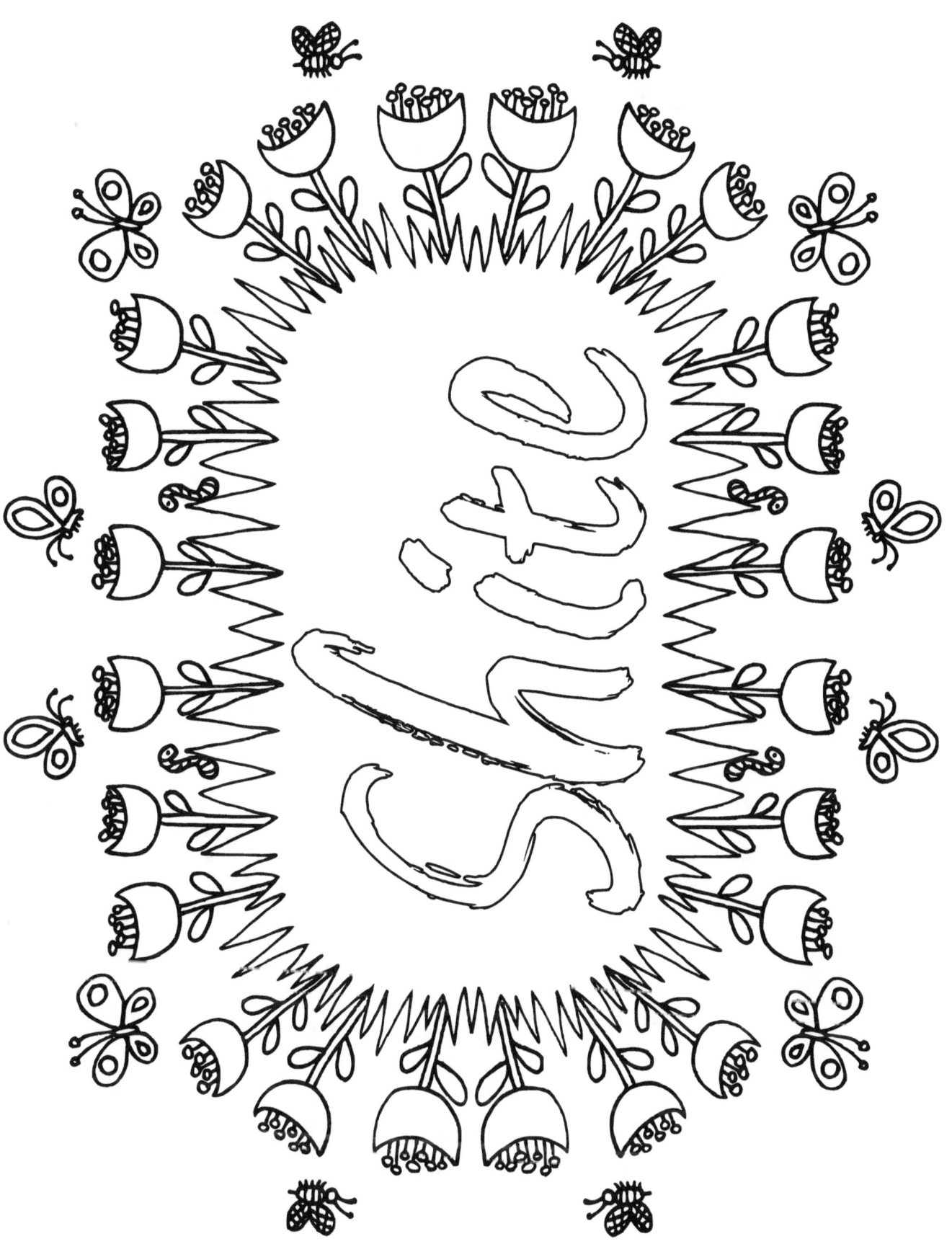

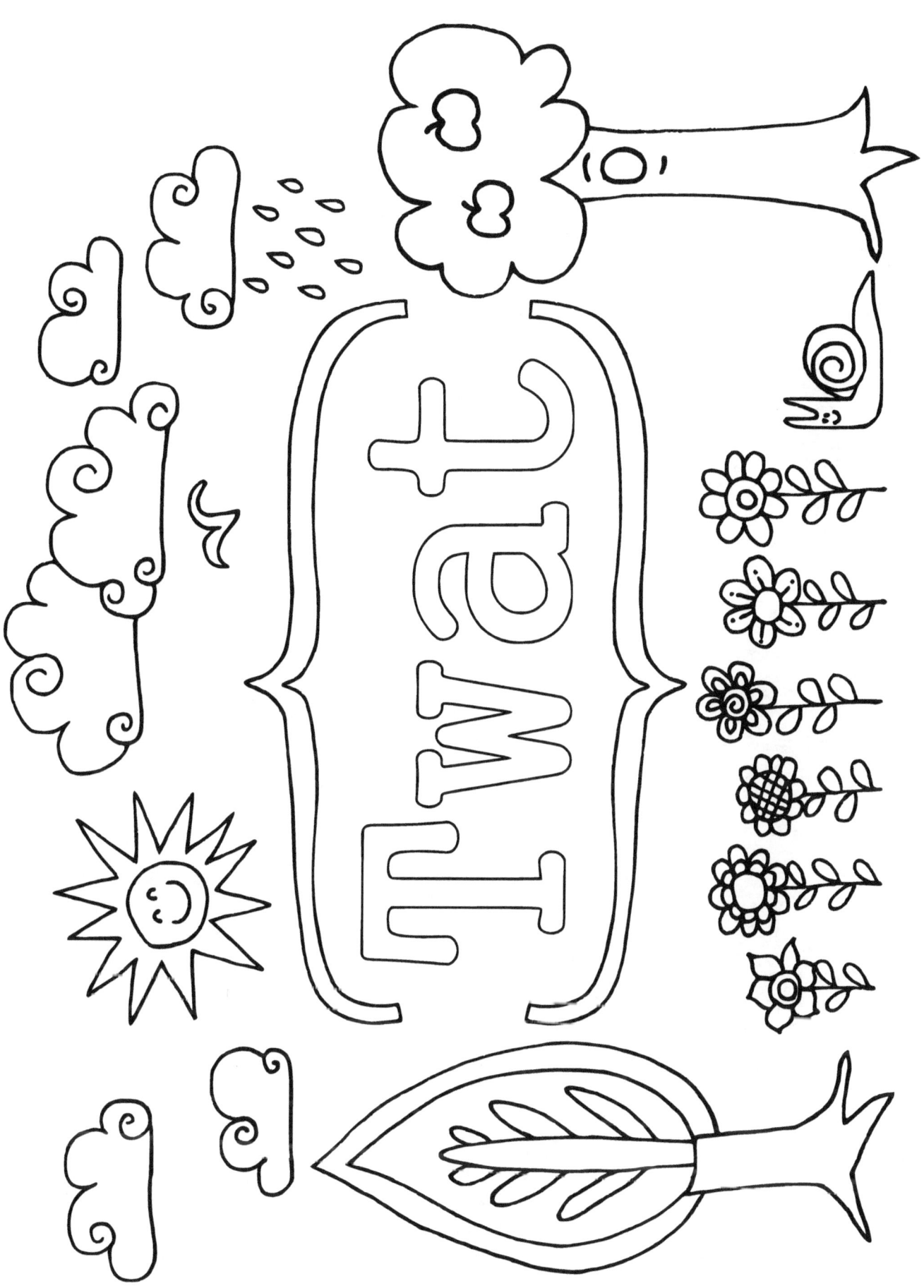

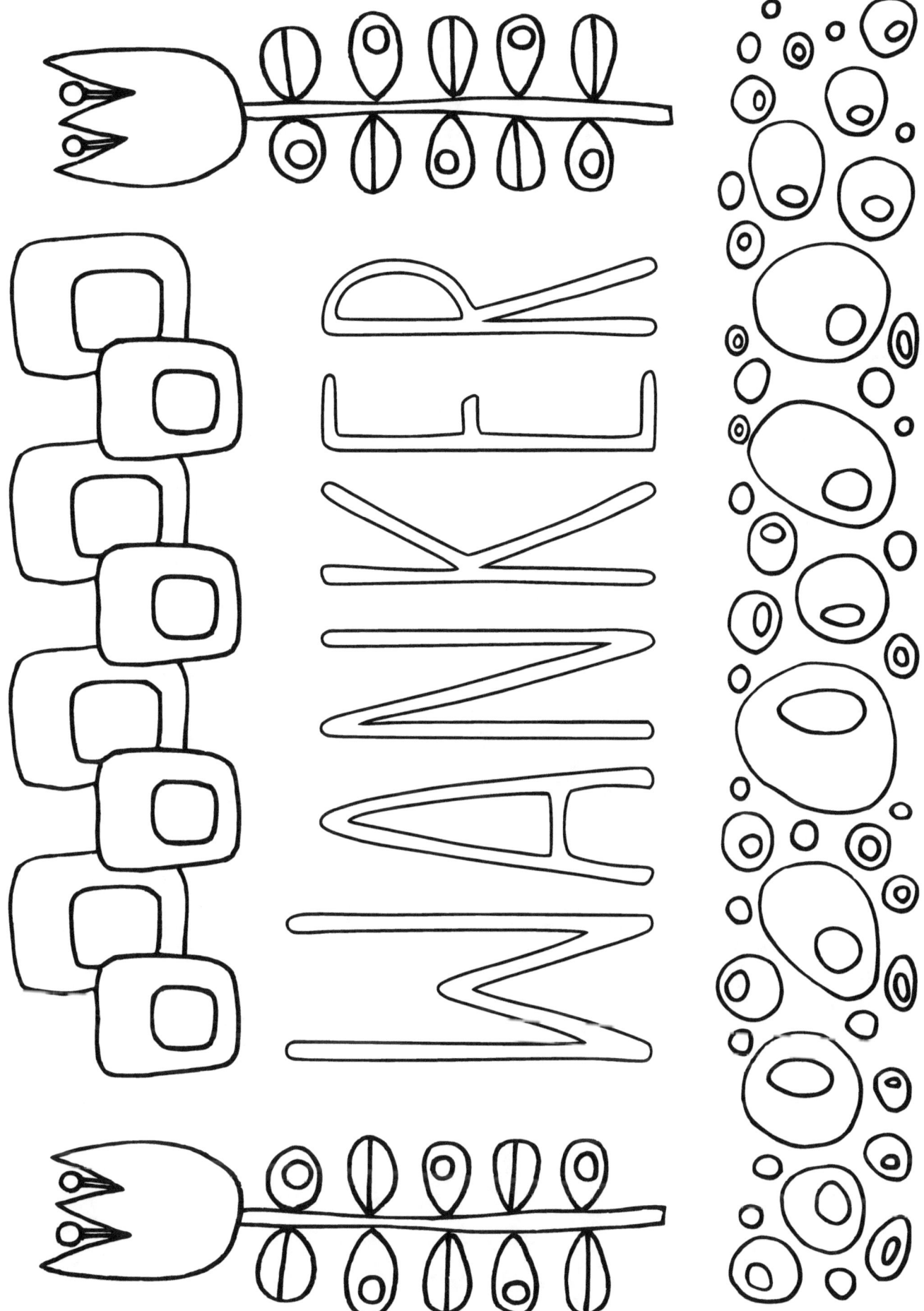

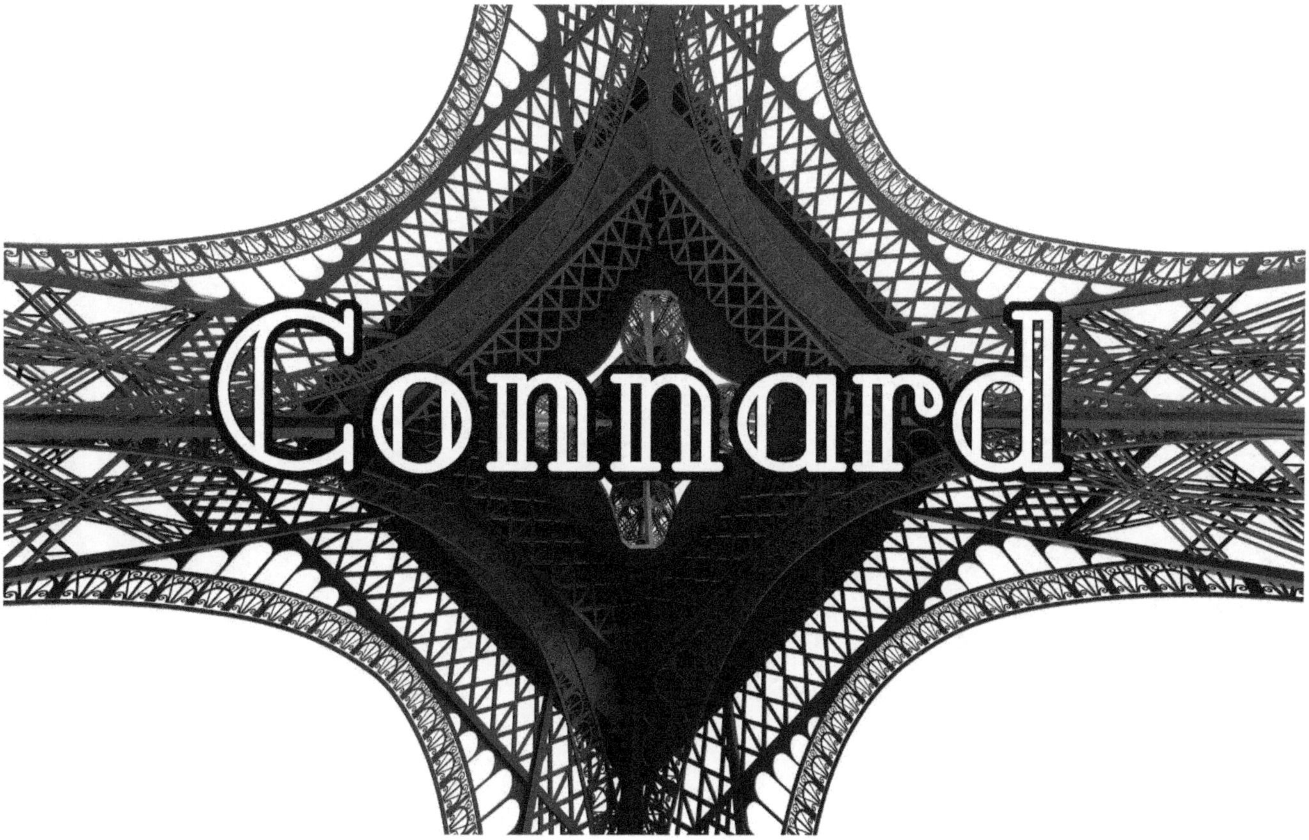

Connard

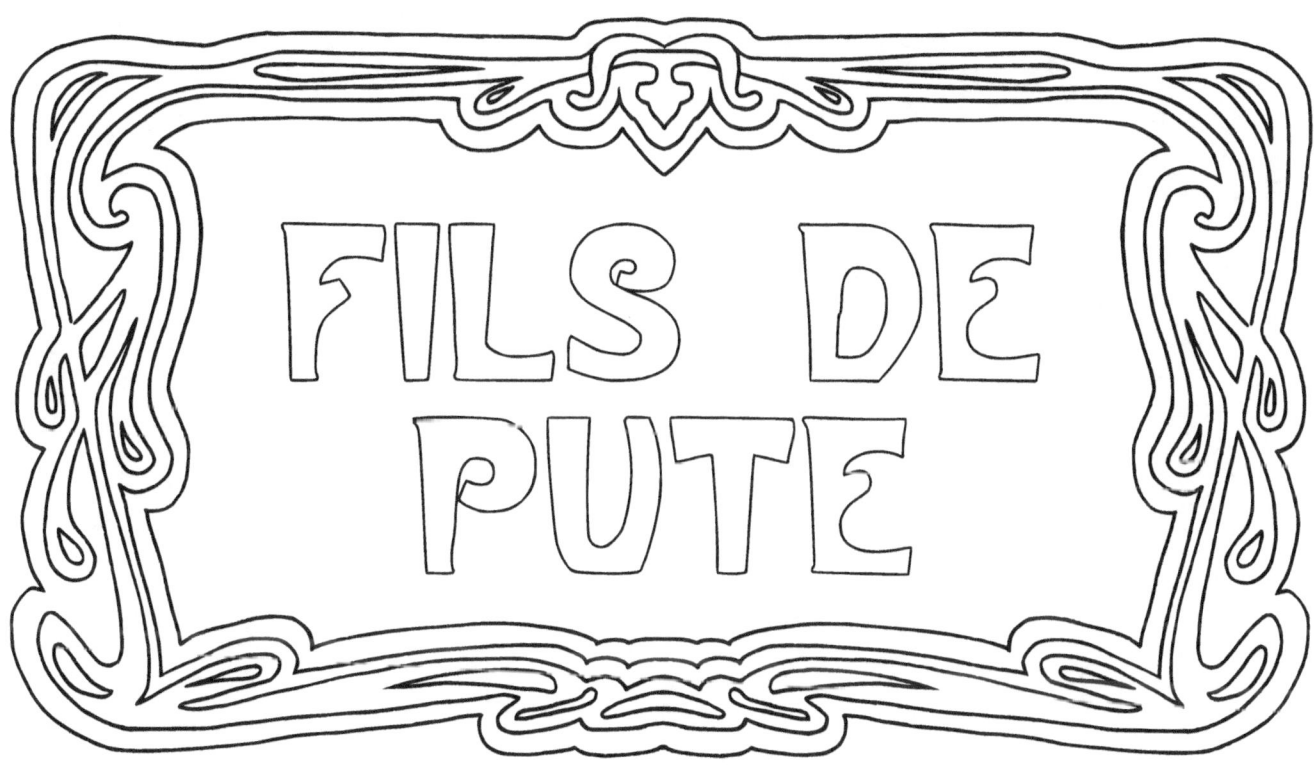

FILS DE PUTE

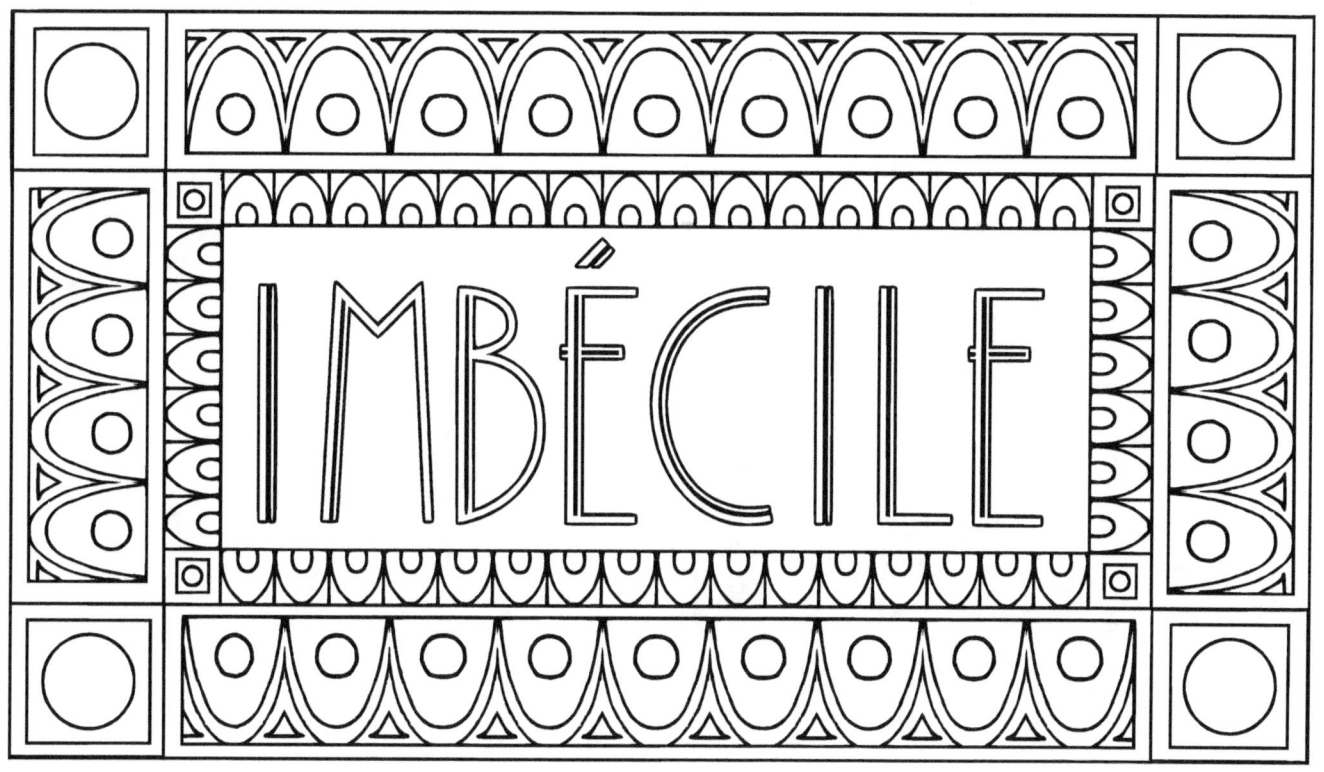

IMBÉCILE

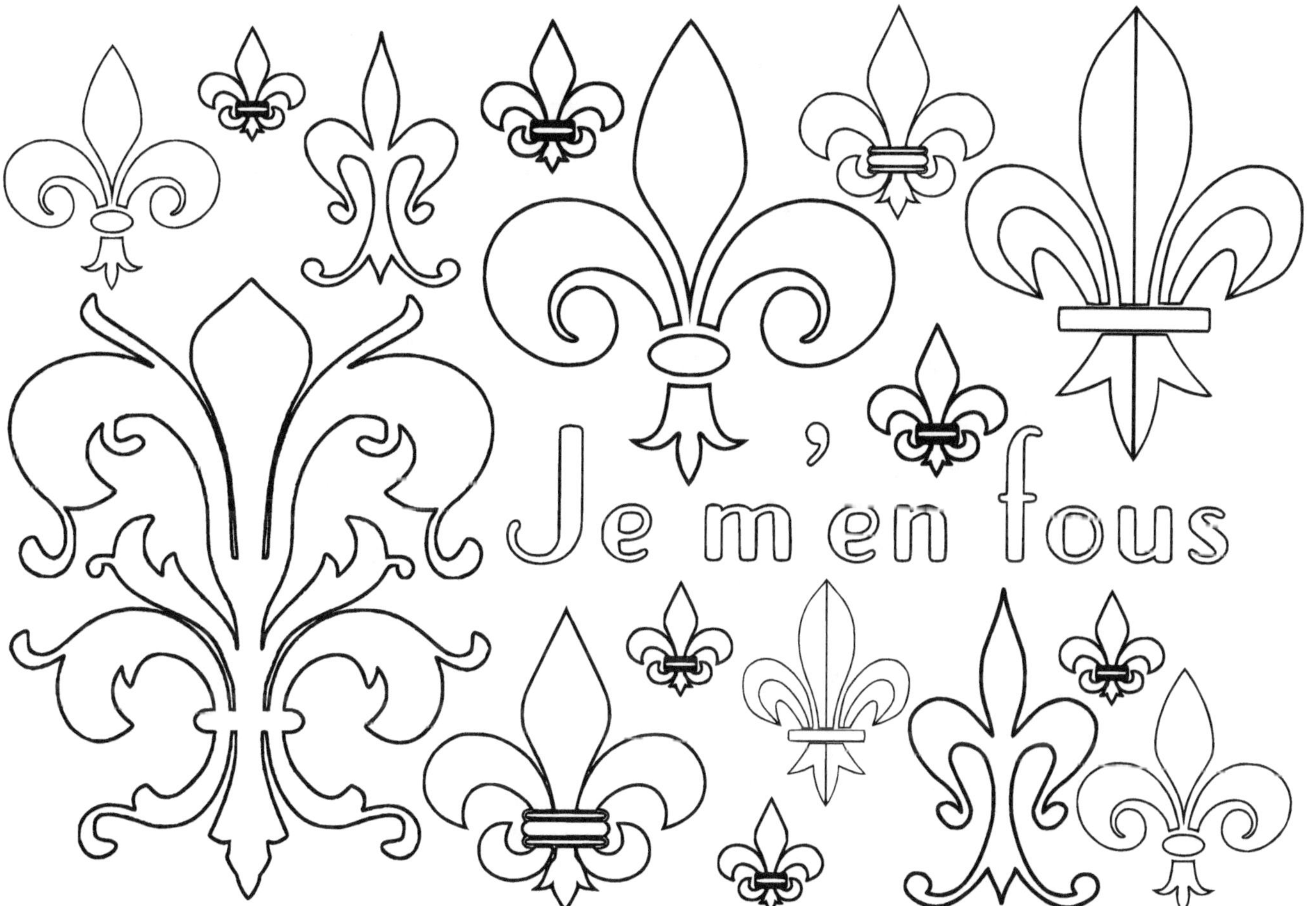

Je m'en fous

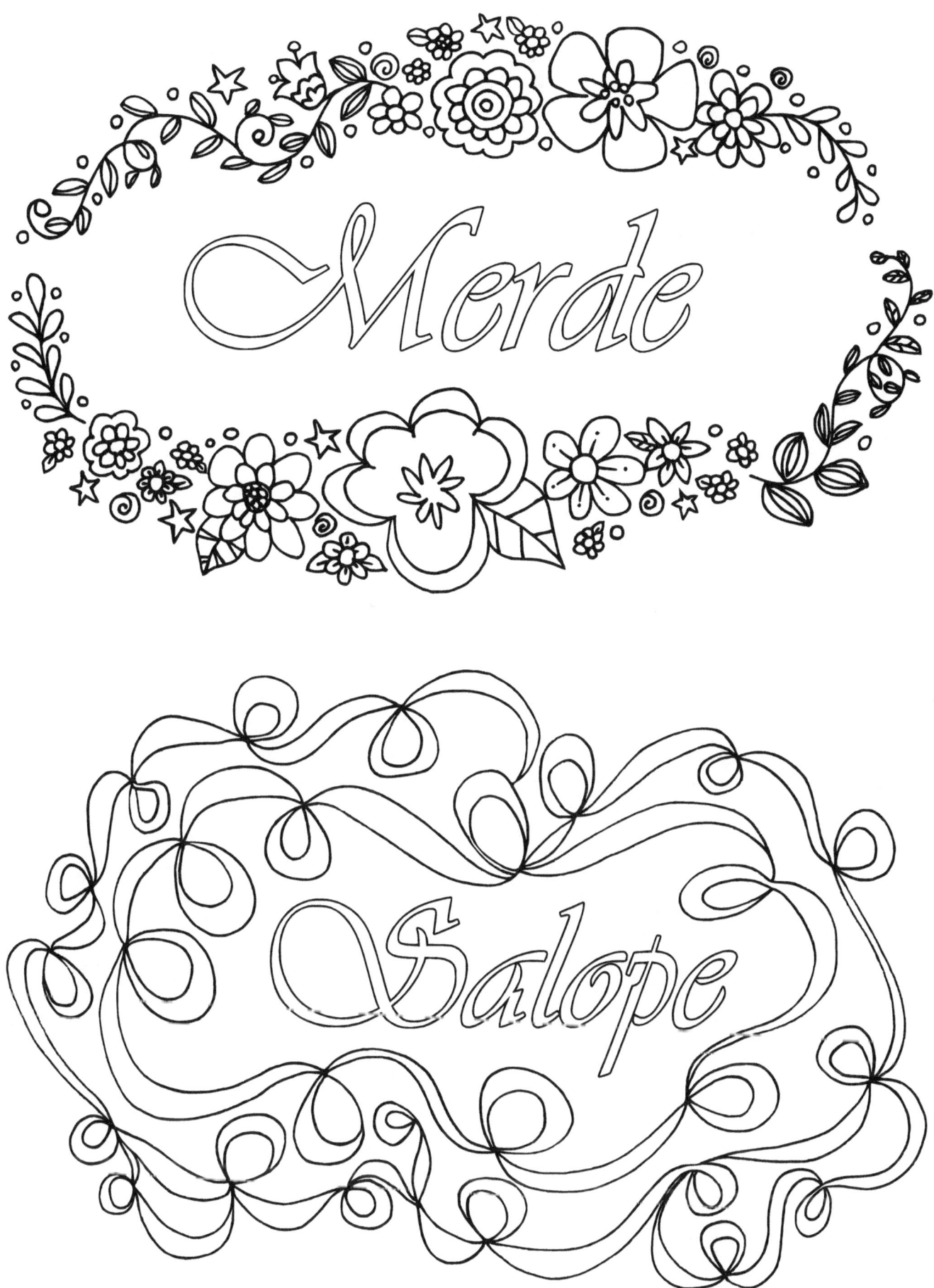

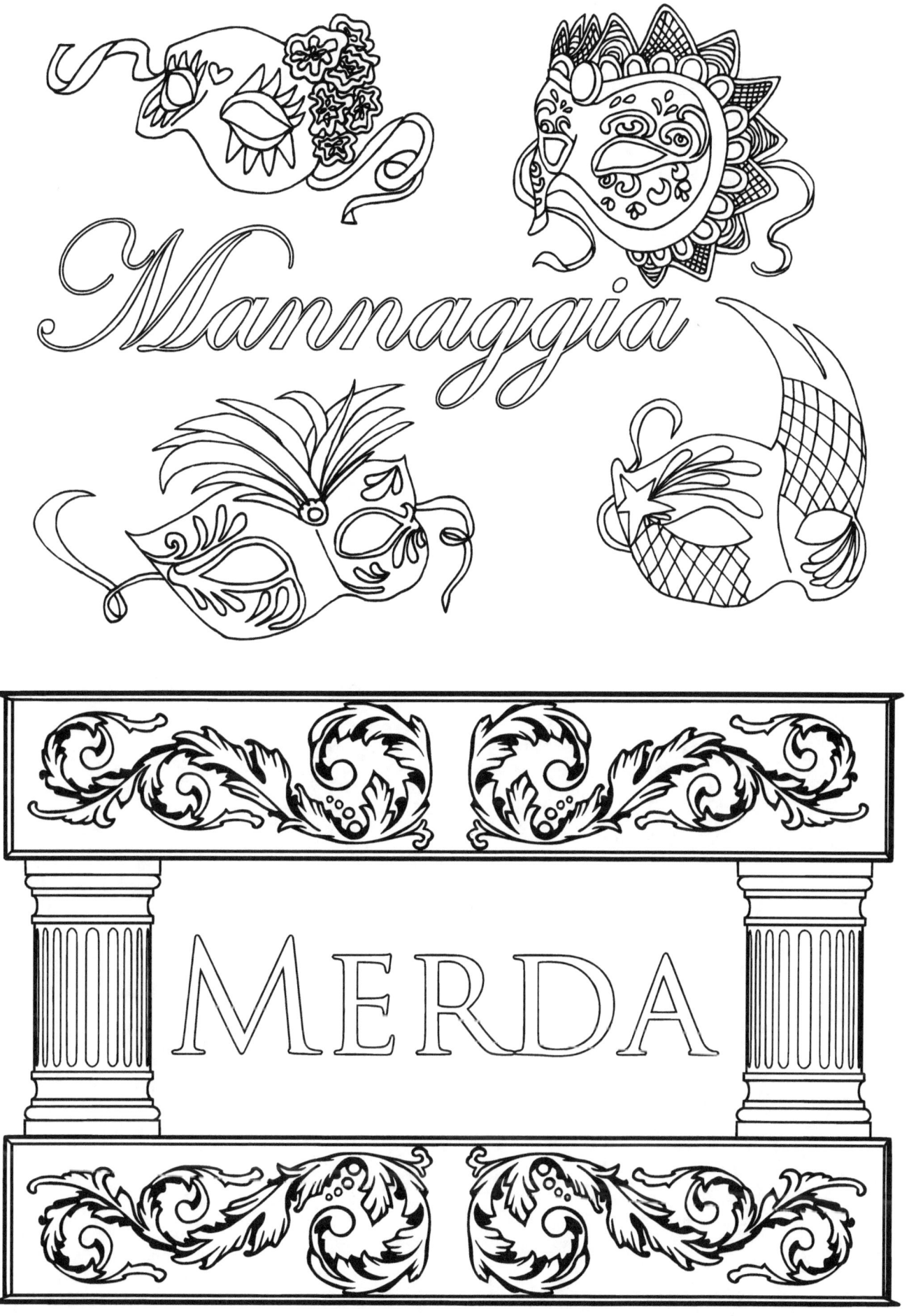

Mannaggia

Merda

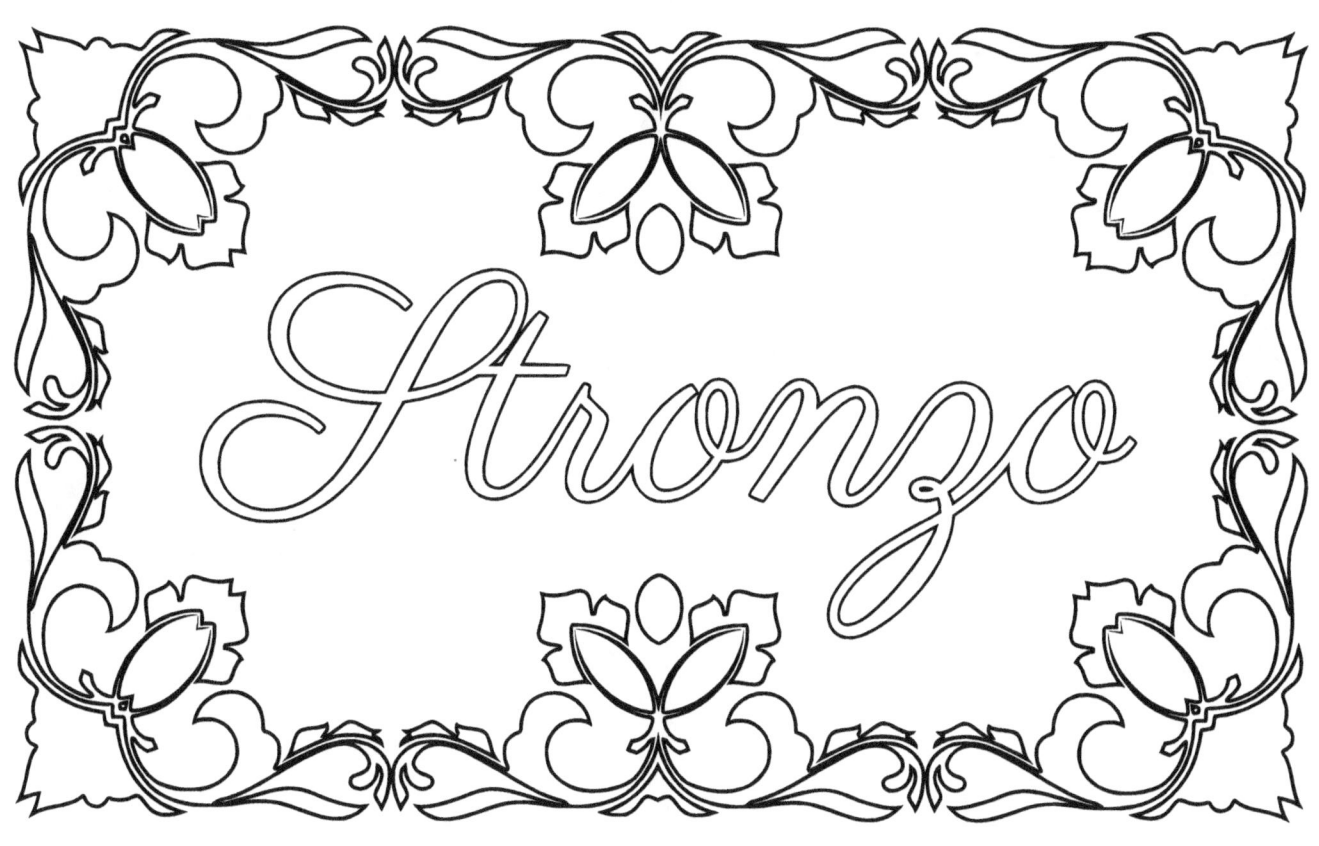

Stronzo

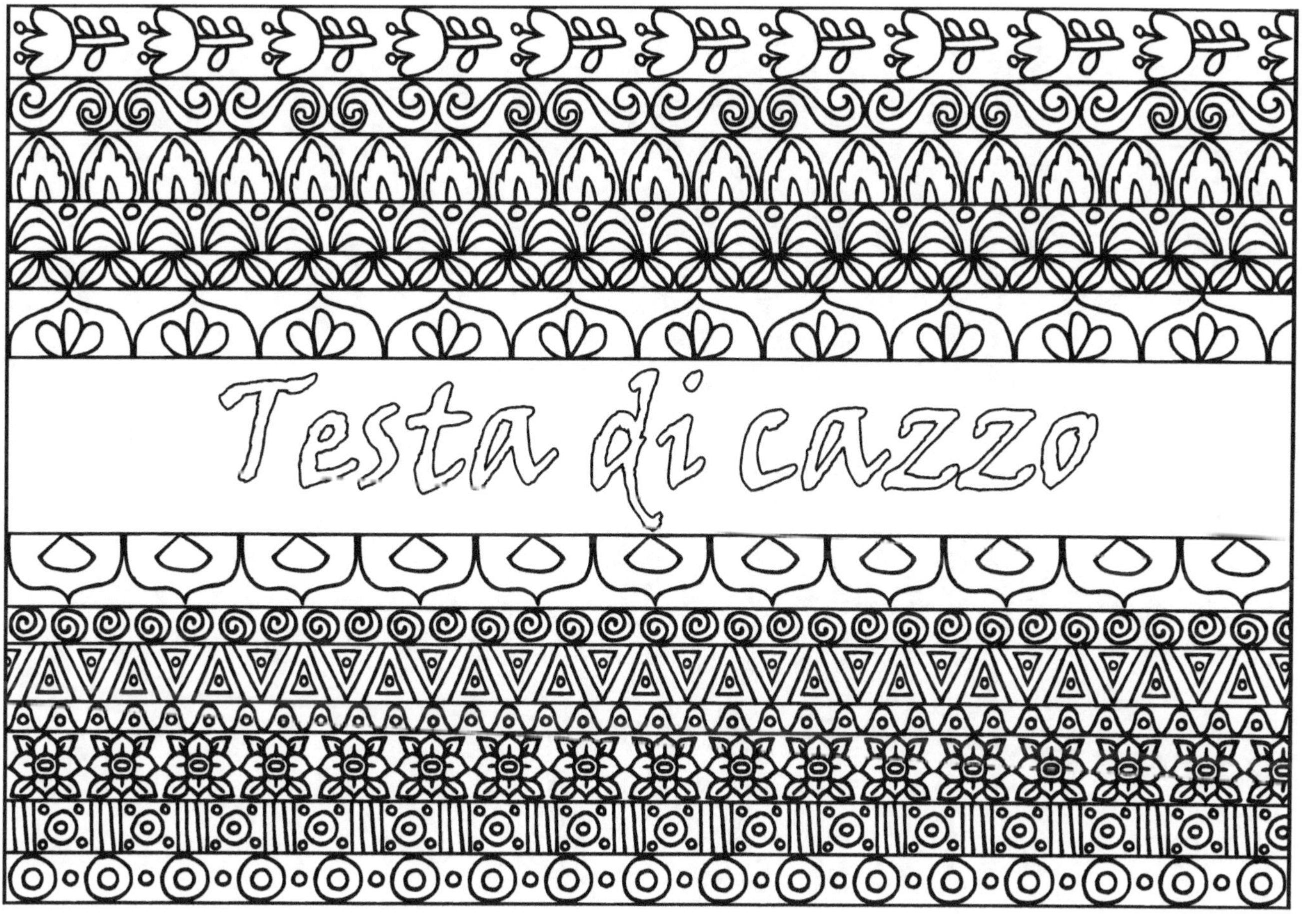

Testa di cazzo

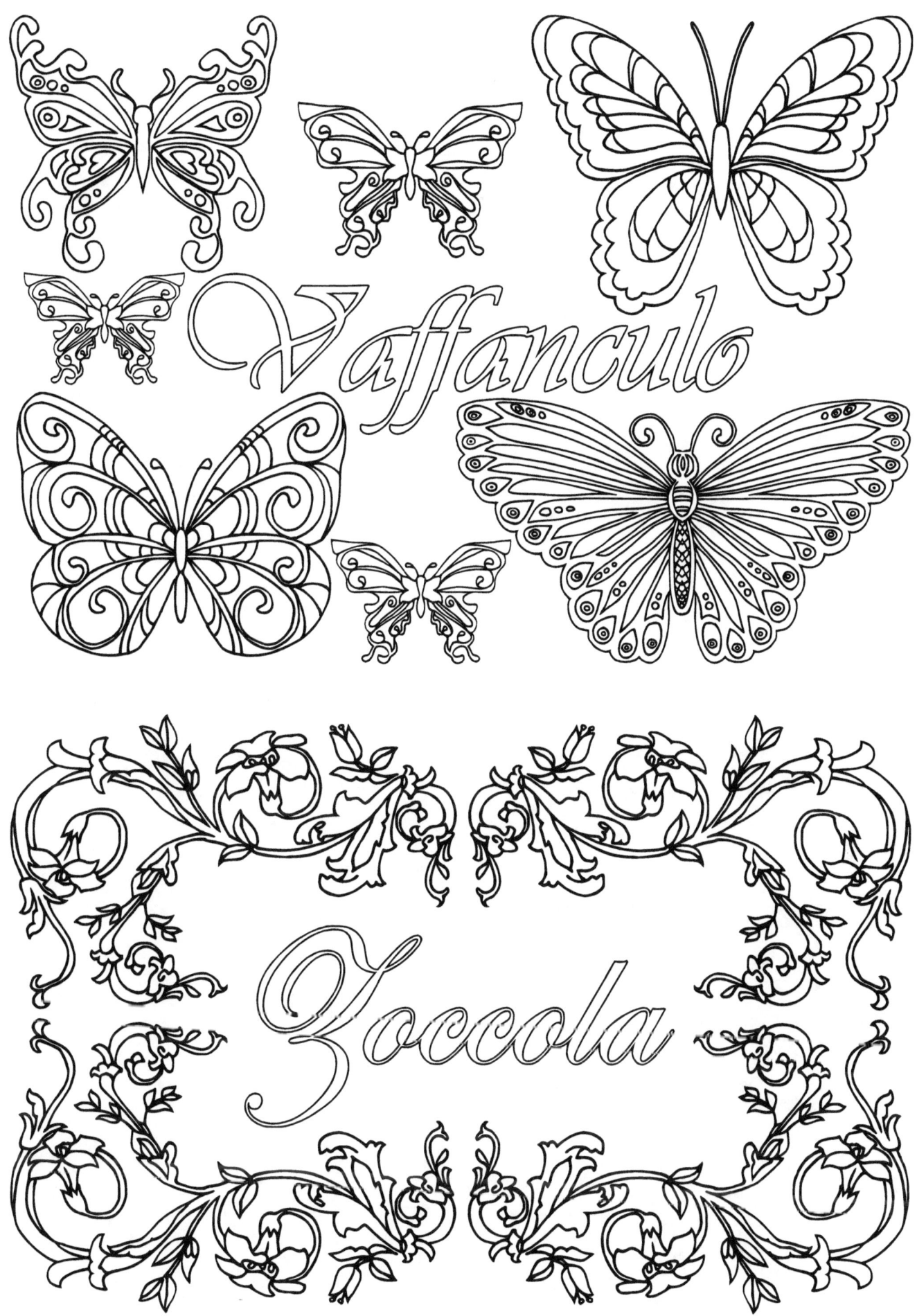

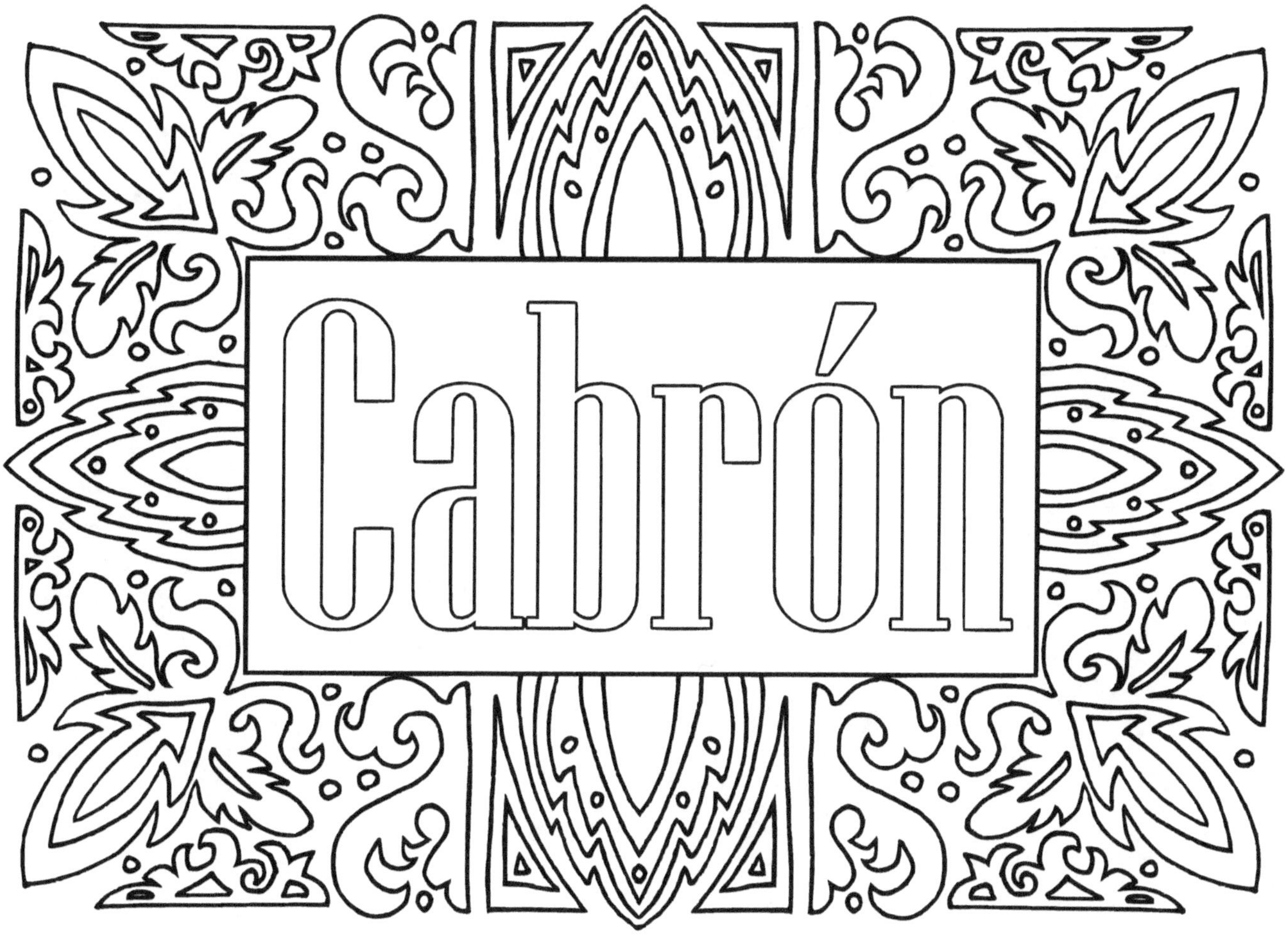

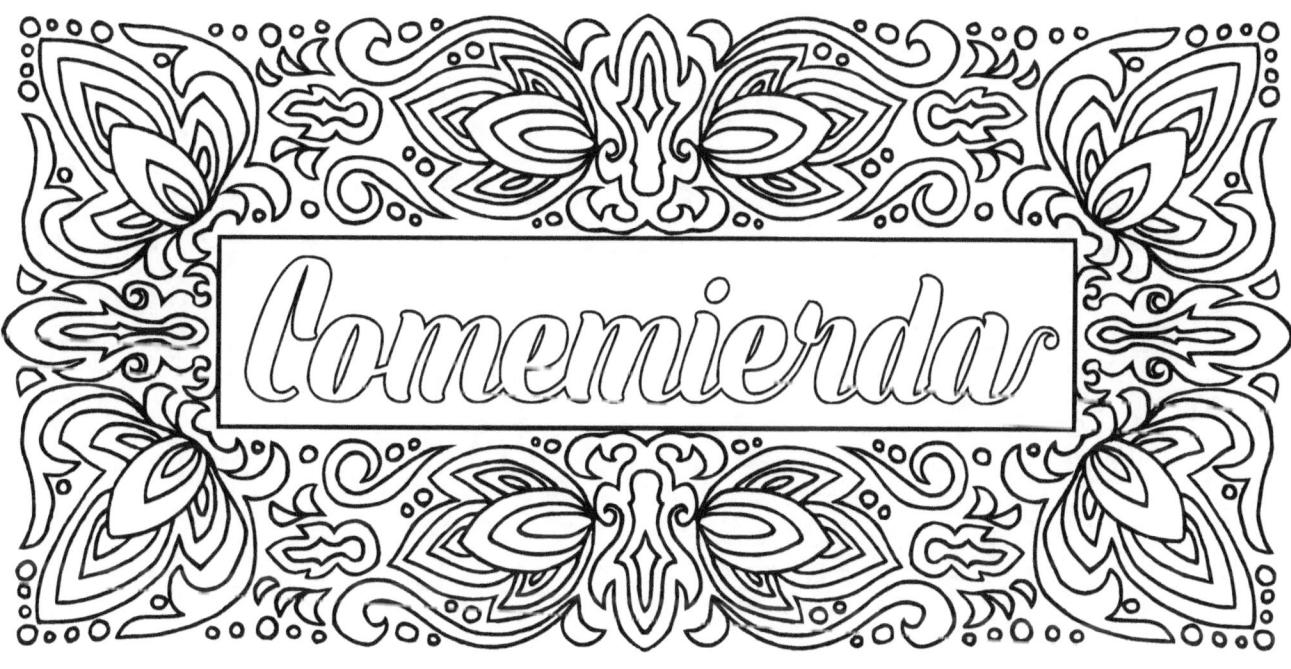

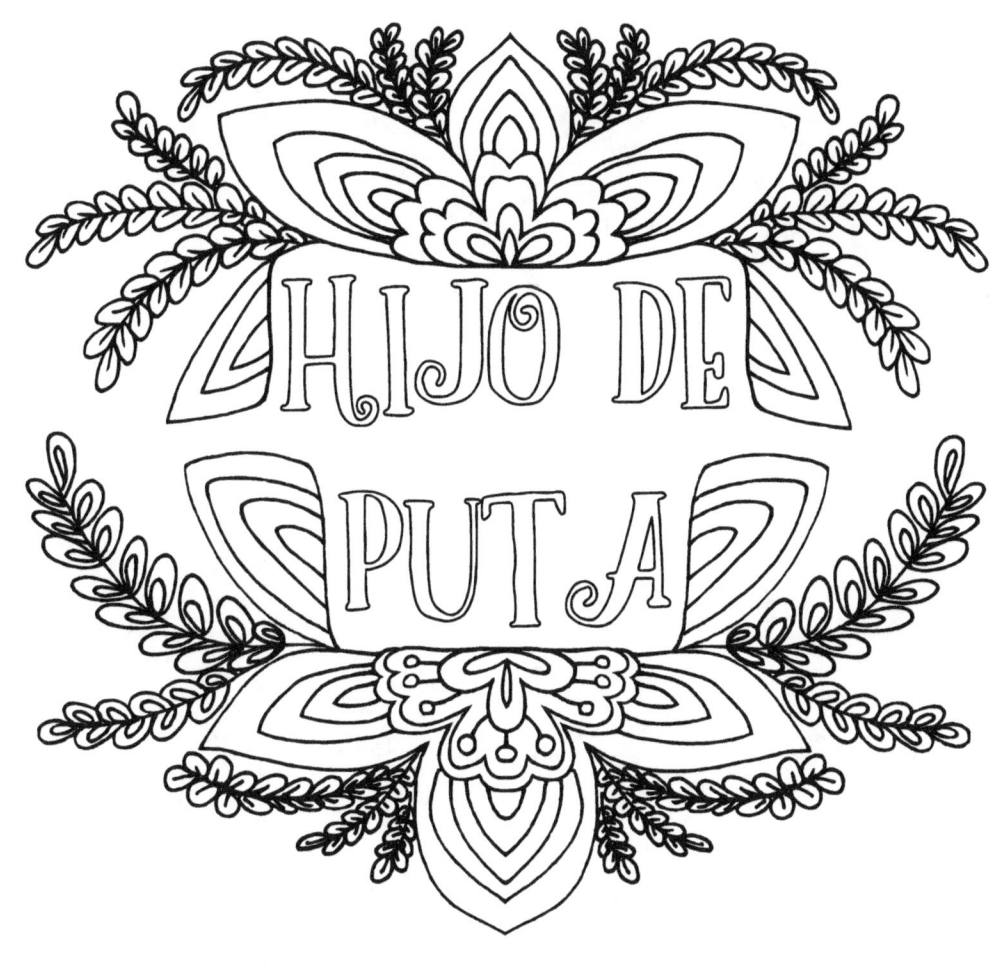

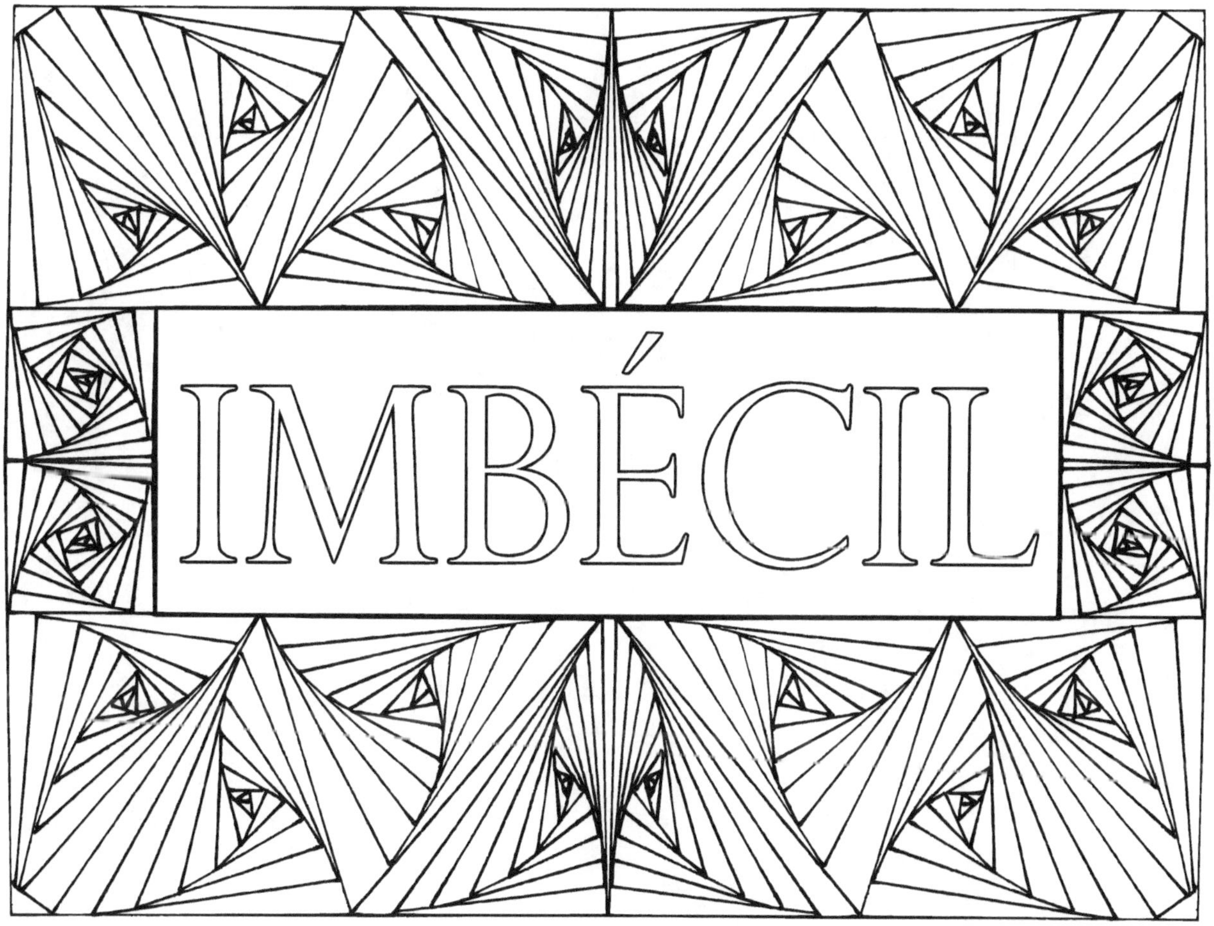

IMBÉCIL

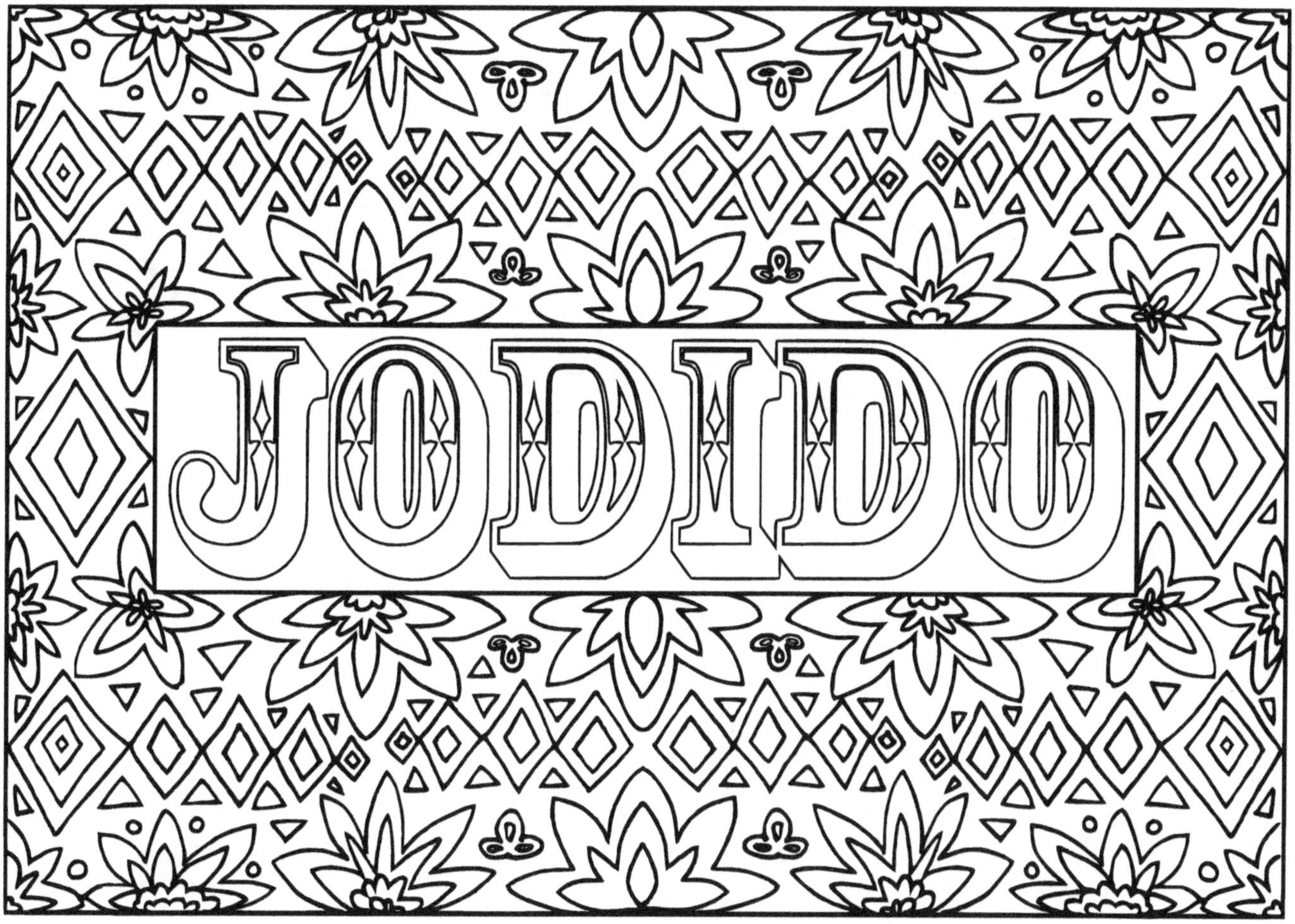

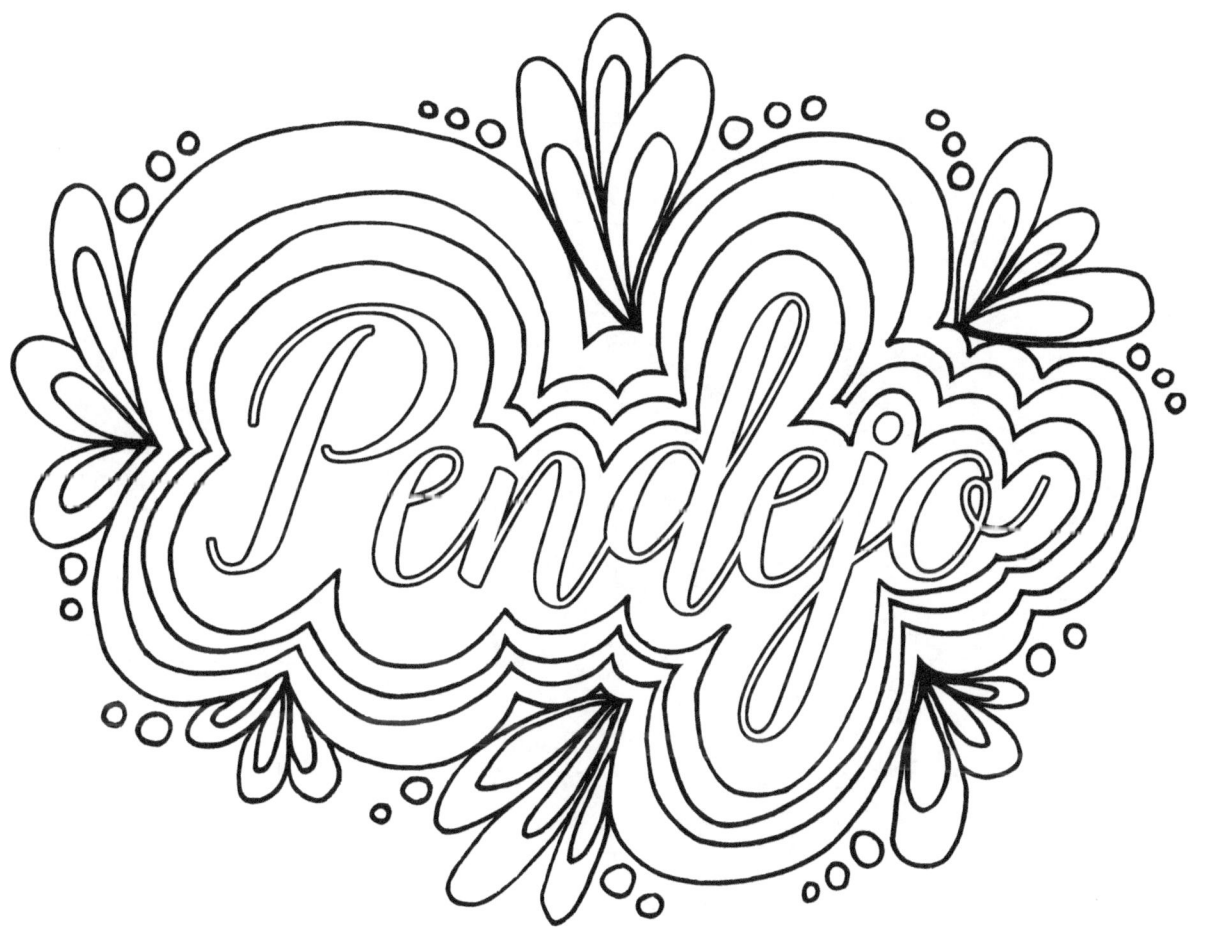

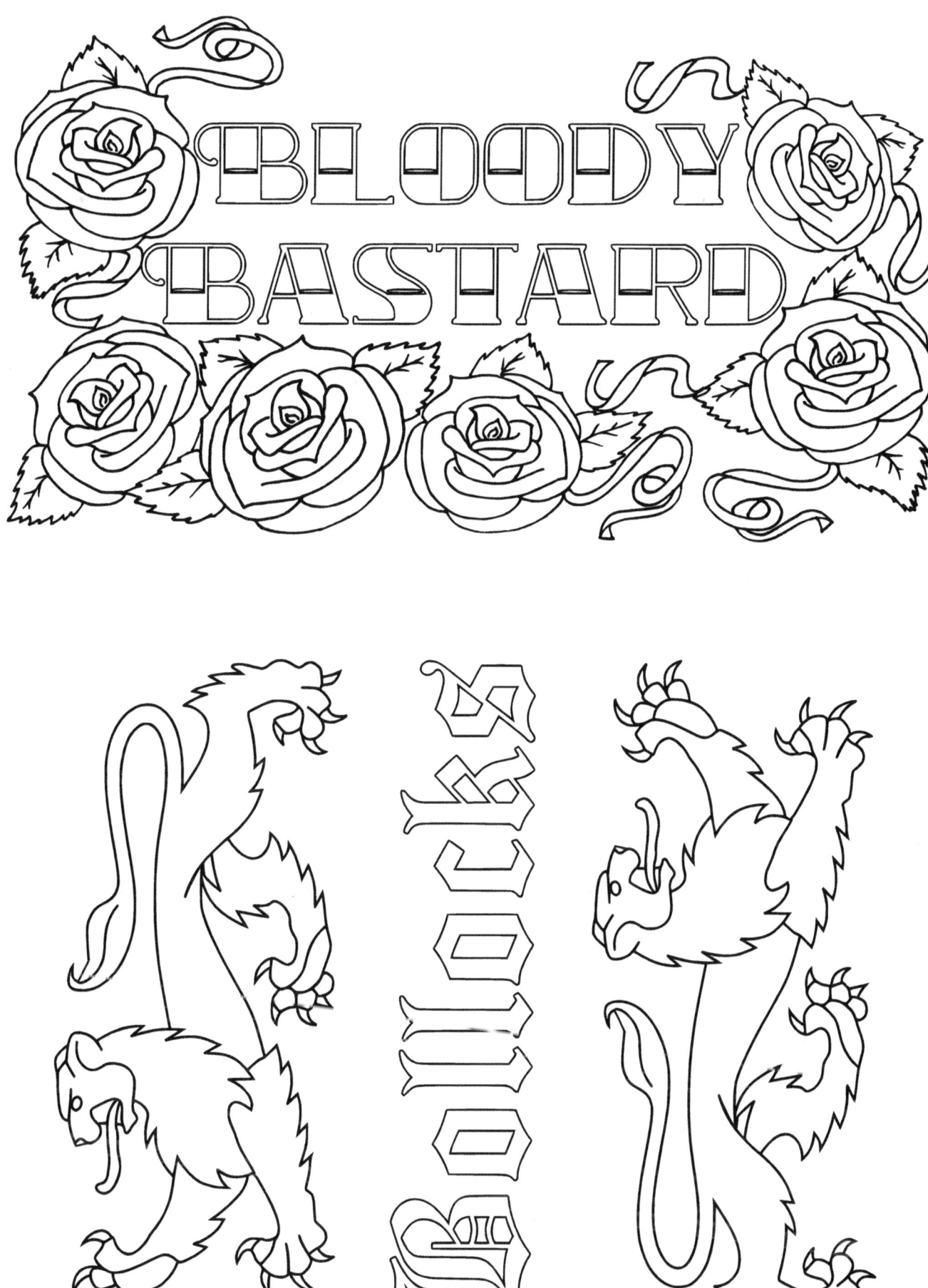

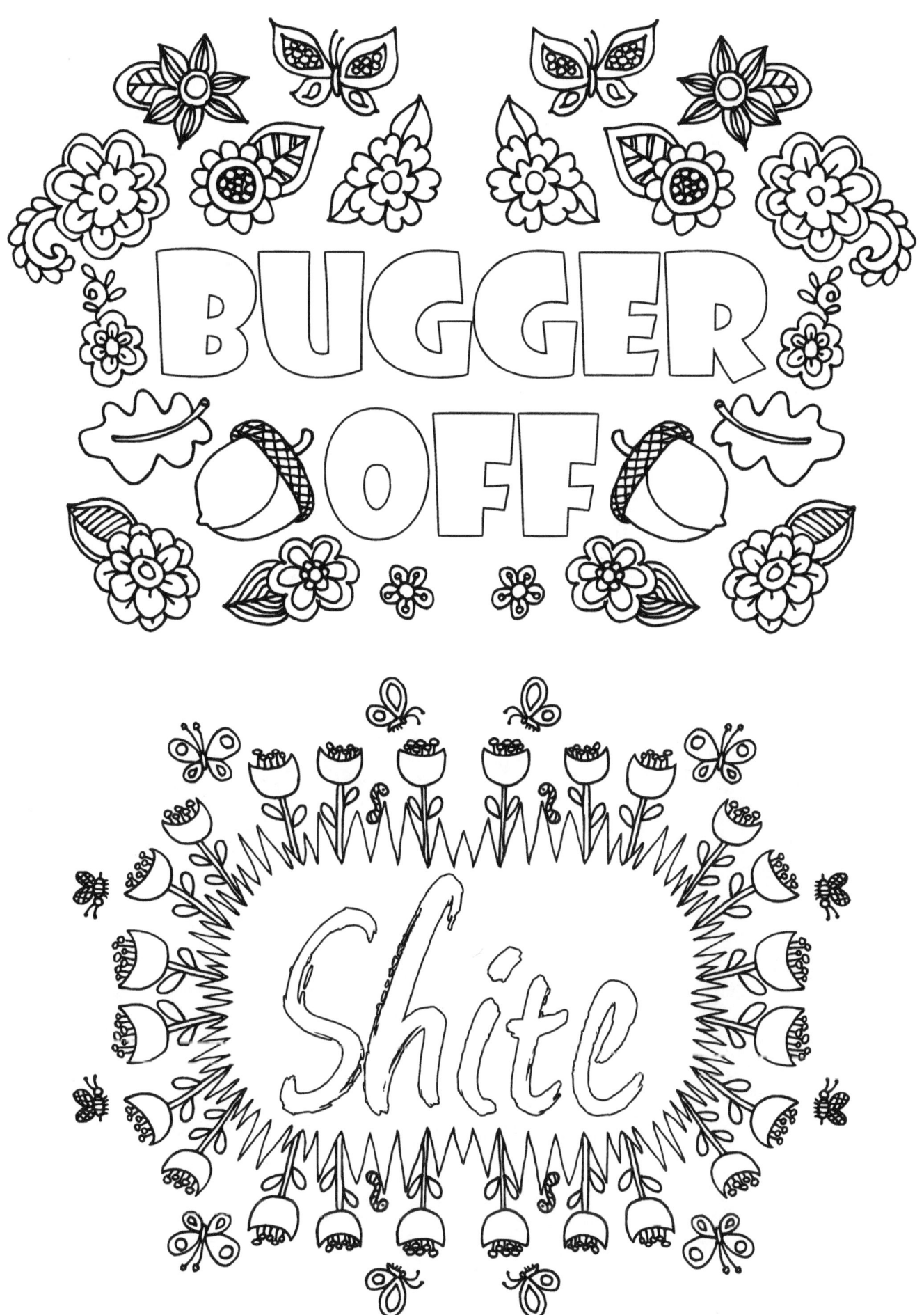

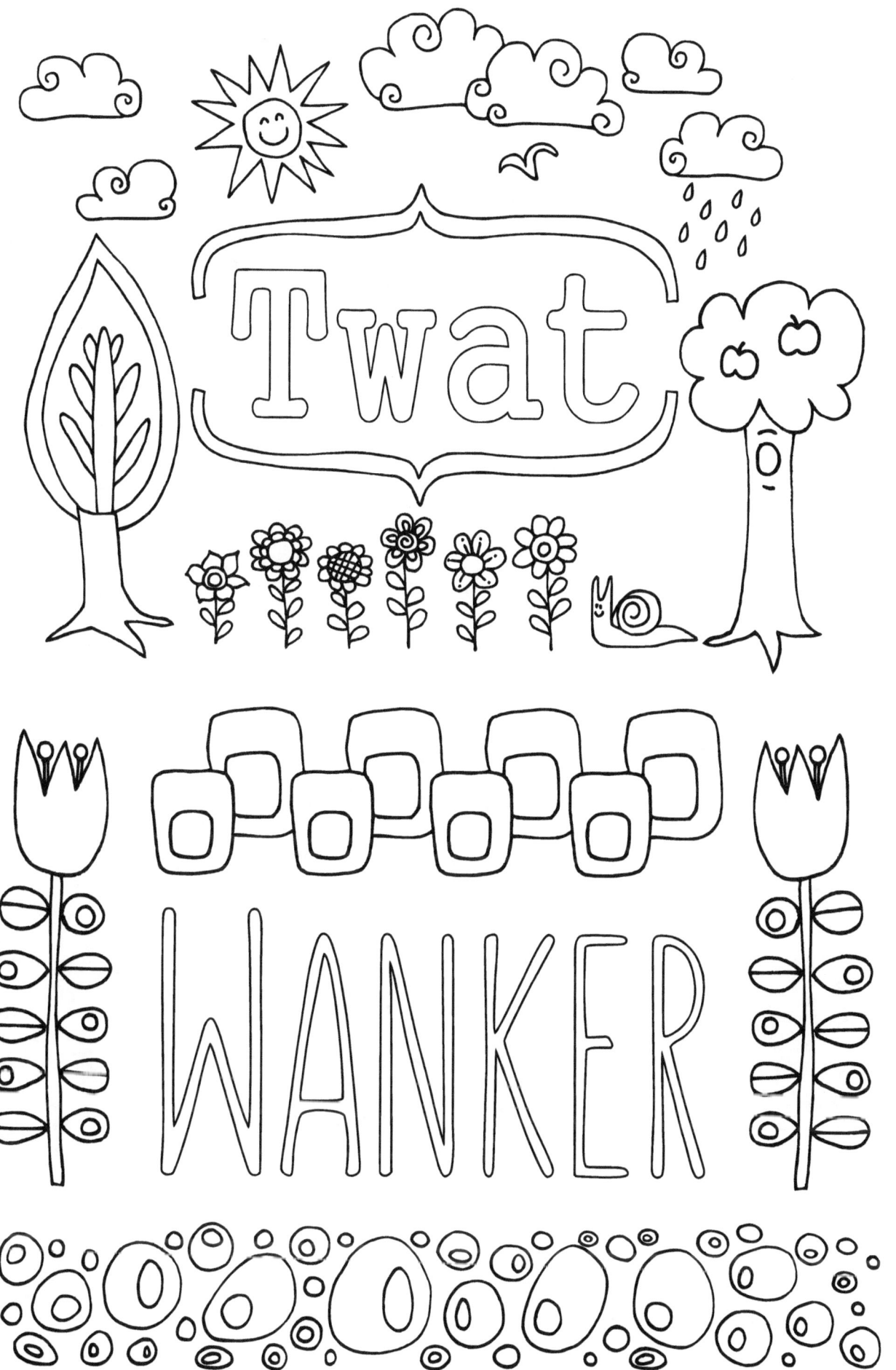

GLOSSARY

French

Connard – Shithead.

Fils de pute - Son of a bitch.

Imbécile - Idiot, moron, jerk.

Je m'en fous - I don't give a fuck.

Merde – Shit.

Salope - Bitch, whore.

Italian

Mannagia – Dammit.

Merda – Shit.

Stronzo – Asshole.

Testa di cazzo – Dickhead.

Vaffanculo - Fuck off, fuck you, go fuck yourself. Literal translation: to take it in the ass.

Zoccola - Bitch, whore. Literal translation: female sewer rat.

Spanish

Cabrón - This is quite the versatile word, with various meanings including son of a bitch, bastard, asshole. Literal translation is male goat, but it means cuckold (a man whose female partner has been unfaithful.) This word's level of insult depends on which country you use it in, from a casual greeting in some countries to quite scathing in others.

Comemierda - Asshole, dumbass. Literally translates to shit-eater and its exact meaning is untranslatable.

Hijo de puta - Son of a bitch.

Imbécil - Idiot, moron, jerk.

Jodido - Fucking, shitty. This word is an intensifier a lot like the word fucking is used in conjunction with other words to intensify them and also used as an exclamation, for example if you slam your hand in a car door.

Pendejo - Motherfucker, coward, dumbass.

British English

Bloody bastard - Despicable or vicious person. Bloody is an ancient swear word that is used as an intensifier a lot like the word fucking is used in conjunction with other words to intensify them. Bastard literally means someone born out of wedlock, but nowadays it's a vicious or despicable person, someone who evokes strong negative feelings.

Bollocks - Bullshit. Literally means testicles, this word is a highly flexible term for something nonsensical, rubbish, or a falsehood.

Bugger off - Fuck off, go away, move on.

Shite - Shit, literally means to defecate.

Twat - Idiot, literally translates to vagina, but used commonly as a more offensive way of saying idiot.

Wanker - Idiot, stupid, annoying person. Literally means someone who masturbates but now is used as a way to express a contemptible person rather than someone's sexual habits.